POLITICAL CORRECTNESS

*The
Cloning
of the
American Mind*

POLITICAL
CORRECTNESS

David Thibodaux, Ph.D.

HUNTINGTON HOUSE PUBLISHERS

Huntington House Publishers
P. O. Box 53788
Lafayette, Louisiana 70505

Quality Trade Paper ISBN 1-56384-026-X
Hardcover ISBN 1-56384-033-2
Library of Congress Card Catalog Number
Quality Trade Paper 92-70281
Hardcover 92-81308

This book is dedicated to my lovely wife, Melody, who brought light and laughter back into my life; to my beautiful children, Ben, Shannon, Jeremy, and Claire, who have brought joy to my life; and to my parents, who are the wind beneath my wings.

Contents

ACKNOWLEDGMENTS

I would like to acknowledge all my colleagues in the professoriate (PC and otherwise) who defend my right to have and to express my opinion, to all my colleagues in my department who have always made me feel free to do so, and especially to Dr. Gary Marotta, Dr. Burton Raffel, Dr. Albert Fields, Dr. Darrell Bourque, Dr. Carl Wooton, Dr. Ann Dobie, and Dr. Joe Andriano, whose assistance, encouragment, and support have meant more to me than I can ever adequately express. I would also like to thank my "lounge buddies," Dr. Joe Riehl, Dr. Mickey Byrd, Dr. Herb Fackler, Dr. Harry Bruder, and Dr. Jim Cox for helping me to keep my "sword sharp and polished."

Chapter 1

POLITICAL CORRECTNESS

Did you know that a man and a woman having a candlelight dinner is considered prostitution?

Did you know that the list of "great literature" was put together by "high-Anglican a—h— to underwrite their social class?"

Did you know that the Constitution of the United States of America is "the embodiment of the White Male with Property Model?"

Did you know that history is "what is important to you?"

Did you know that any piece of writing "has so many different meanings that it has no meaning" at all?

Did you know that the "real" Son of God was black and was born four thousand years before Jesus?

If any of these points strike you as odd, welcome to the wonderful world of political correctness.

A little over one year ago, a conference entitled "Political Correctness and Cultural Studies" was held at Berkeley. "Like tie-dyed T-shirts," said Robert L. Caserio, an associate professor of English at the University of Utah and one of the organizers of the conference, "political correctness on today's campus is making a comeback from the 1960's" (*Chronicle*, 21 November 1990, p. A-14). As the name of the conference ("Political Correctness and Cultural Studies") suggests, there are offshoots of the original movement which have come to be known by different names. Some of the "isms" spawned by political correctness are "multiculturalism" (see chap. 2), "Afrocentrism" (see chap. 3), and "genderism," which is a new name for radical "feminism" (see chap. 4). Nevertheless, according to the *Chronicle of Higher Education* there is general agreement that political correctness (and all its attendant "isms") "grew out of the social and political movements of the 1960s and has been associated with the left in academe" (28 November 1990, p. A-5). It has been called "a new fundamentalism," and "the new fundamentalists are an eclectic group; they include multiculturalists, feminists, [and 'genderists'], radical homosexuals, Marxists, and New Historicists" (*New York Magazine*, 21 January 1991, p. 34).

The 1992 *Britannica World Data* Annual contains the following comments on political correctness:

> The origins of the phrase "politically correct" are obscure. Some trace it to Mao Tse-Tung. . . . In 1975 Karen DeCrow, then the president of the National Organization for Women, told critics that NOW was moving in an "intellectually and politically correct direction." But it has also been claimed that the term appeared as early as the 1960s to refer in an ironic or derisive manner to people who tailored their views to fit prevailing political fashions.
>
> Whatever its origins, the phrase "politically correct" acquired a new vogue in the late 80s when it began to be used, first on college campuses and later by the media, as a pejorative term to describe a loose collection of feminists, Marxists, multiculturalists, and deconstructionists together with their assorted left-wing positions on race, sexual orientation, gender, class, the environment, and related issues. It was considered politically correct, for example, to recycle newspaper, to oppose the wearing of fur coats, to decry American capitalism and consumerism, to abhor the pernicious influence of advertising and television, to support a woman's right to an abortion, to use the term "Native American" instead of "Indian" and "African-American" instead of "black." On a larger scale, politically correct

thinking included the view that American history is
primarily a narrative of exploitation and oppression,
and that Americans ought to celebrate the "other-
ness" or "difference" of the women, homosexuals,
and ethnic groups who had long been denied a voice
by the white males who traditionally controlled
Western society.

The most controversial feature of politically correct behavior, however, was an inclination to suppress, or at least vociferously condemn, books and
viewpoints and even social activities that, regardless
of how innocuous, were believed to be racist or
sexist. (p. 459)

As Don Feder, a nationally syndicated columnist
pointed out in an article in the *Washington Times*, "The
apologia for political correctness alternately maintains (1)
political correctness does not exist, or (2) if it does exist,
the phenomenon is grossly overstated, or (3) if not exaggerated, it really isn't so bad" (4 October 1991). It is
said that all evidence of such a phenomenon is "anecdotal"
and that these isolated incidents reported in such publications as the *Chronicle of Higher Education* are insuf-
ficient evidence upon which to base the conclusion that
a national movement is underway. This argument was, in
fact, stated by a colleague of mine during a panel discussion on our campus.

My department (English) has an annual meeting called
the Professional Colloquium, the purpose of which is to
discuss some issue of interest to those of us in higher
education. Attendance at the Colloquium (English 500)
is required of the graduate students in the department. The
1991-92 Colloquium featured a panel of professors who
were gathered together to discuss the phenomenon of
political correctness. It was during this panel discussion
that one of my colleagues made the comment that all the
evidence of a national movement known as political correctness was "anecdotal." My response was that, first of
all, my colleague was incorrect in that there is, indeed, *all*

kinds of evidence, not *just* anecdotal, that this movement is real and widespread. That notwithstanding, I went on to say that my colleague was correct in that while not *all* of the evidence is "anecdotal," as he called it, much of it is, but that does not make it insignificant or irrelevant for "anecdotal evidence" is like unto "circumstantial evidence." Of circumstantial evidence, Chief Justice Earl Warren once said that each piece of such evidence is like a thread; given enough pieces of thread, one can make a quilt.

This book is a patchwork quilt of incidents from all across this nation which will provide a very clear indication of some of the theories and notions that are being pushed in public education today, and there are more than enough examples and anecdotes to make a very impressive quilt, i.e., to establish very clearly that political correctness, or "PC" as it has come to be called, is a bonafide movement which is very broad in scope. In addition, I will provide further evidence, anecdotal and otherwise, to prove that the PC movement is no longer confined to college campuses; it has found its way into the political arena and has also trickled down into our secondary and elementary schools.

There is hardly an issue of the *Chronicle of Higher Education* in the last year-and-a-half that does not have at least one article about this subject. Political correctness has become so widespread and controversial that the American Association of University Professors (AAUP) and the Modern Language Association (MLA) have felt compelled to issue statements concerning this phenomenon. It has become the subject of comic strips, and feature stories on PC and its attendant "isms" have appeared in such publications as *Time, Newsweek,* and *New York Magazine.* Even ABC's "Nightline" devoted an entire show to the impact that political correctness and multiculturalism has had on the teaching of history. Furthermore, Professor Everette E. Dennis of Columbia University stated in a speech delivered as the 1991 fall

Convocation Lecture at the University of Oregon, "I have been surprised to learn how far this controversy has spread. During several trips to East and Central Europe, the Balkans and the Soviet Union [now defunct], I have often been asked both about political correctness and multiculturalism," which Professor Dennis calls "the conceptual companion in the campus debate" of political correctness (*The War of the Words: Freedom of Expression, the University and the Media,* The Freedom Forum Media Studies Center, Columbia University, Fall 1991, pp. 6-7).

The politically correct movement has been called "a fascism of the left" and a "left-wing McCarthyism," which is characterized by "a radical anti-Americanism." Its proponents have been accused of "allowing their political agenda to taint their scholarship and teaching." One of the goals on that agenda (its principle one, according to John Silber, president of Boston University) is not only to challenge the ascendancy of Western culture, but to vilify that culture.

According to the *Chronicle of Higher Education,* political correctness has resulted in "the polarization of the academy into opposing camps. . . . The polarization is most intense in the humanities and social sciences [which is my field]: On one side are scholars who have made issues of race, gender, and class central to their teaching and scholarship. They have been labeled 'politically correct' [or PC for short]." On the other side are scholars who "advocate the study of Western culture and an 'objective' approach to scholarship," and those in this group have been labeled "conservative, right-wing, racist, sexist, homophobes" by the politically correct crowd (*Chronicle,* 30 January 1991, p. A-15). In other words, according to the PC crowd, this group is "politically incorrect." I shall call them PNC for short, and I boldly proclaim my membership in this group, the *in*correct one.

Professor Dennis contends that the politically correct movement is "best understood as 'enlightenment theology,' much like a quasi-religious belief regarding how, as well as what, people should say and think," and that it "sets out to critique the world on transcendental moral grounds" (*War of Words,* p. 7). Professor Caserio of the University of Utah calls political correctness "a prefabricated sense of values, a predetermined set of assumptions about what is good for people and what is bad for them" (*Chronicle,* 21 November 1990, p. A-14). Politically correct academics have been accused "of refusing to question assumptions they held, even when it became apparent that those assumptions were no longer valid" (*Chronicle,* 30 January 1991, p. A-15). Examples would be scholars who have continued to present in their classes Marxist economic models as ideals to pursue, even as the Communist world continues to disintegrate; scholars who continue to refer to the Sandanistas as "heroes" even though they were "overthrown" by the people of Nicaragua in a free election; and scholars who continue to discuss the strengths of Chinese society, even in the wake of Tiananmen Square. Ironically, with what is happening in Communist countries today, the American university campus may be the only place left on earth where one can find an avowed Marxist.

The explanation for the leftist nature of the politically correct movement is as clear as it is simple. As already mentioned, the politically correct movement on campus has much in common with 1960s liberalism, and the reason for this is simply because many of the student activists and radicals of the sixties have found a home in academe and are now faculty members and administrators in the universities. Annette Kolodny, dean of the humanities faculty at the University of Arizona, frankly admitted, "I see my scholarship as an extension of my political activism" (*New York Magazine,* 21 January 1991, p. 36). James A. Berlin, a professor of rhetoric at Purdue University visited my campus recently, and I had the opportunity to meet and speak with him. His position is that the classroom is unavoidably political and that it is critical that such issues be discussed. Prof. Berlin, by the way, is a self-proclaimed Marxist, what he calls a "low-risk" Marxist. Such honest admissions are the exception for the PC crowd, however, because ... as Carl Raschke, Professor of Religious Studies at the University of Denver, maintains, "The American intelligentsia has a tremendous capacity for what psychologists call 'denial' (*Chronicle* 9 Jan. 1991, p. A-3). Professor Dennis points out, "Political correctness . . . while believed by many critics to accurately diagnose a campus condition—some would say 'pathology'—is usually denied by those accused of being at the center of any number of new orthodoxies, from deconstructionist theory to cultural studies" (*War of Words*, p. 7). I believe that Professor Dennis is exactly correct, but to understand his point, one must know what "deconstructionist theory" and "cultural studies" are. As already mentioned, "multiculturalism" and/or "cultural studies" will be discussed in detail in chapter 2, so let us begin with "deconstruction."

A *Handbook to Literature*, edited by C Hugh Holman, which is basically a dictionary of literary terms, defines deconstruction as a "widespread philosophical and critical movement that owes its name and recent energy to the precepts and examples of Jacques Derrida [a French linguist], whose works have been available in English translation since the 1960s" (p. 133). Consider for a moment the following expanded definition of deconstruction from the Holman *Handbook*.

> Perhaps the most important doctrine leading to *deconstruction* is Saussure's [Ferdinand de Saussure] conclusion that "in language there are only differences. Even more important: a difference generally implies positive terms between which the difference is set up: but in language there are only differences *without positive terms*." As the "linguistic model" is extended to describe other systems, the concept of thing, substance, event and absolute recedes, to be superseded by the concept of relation, ratio, con-

struct, and relativity, all covered by Derrida's stimulating coinage "DIFFERANCE," which includes difference, differing, and deferral. Once one realizes that what seems to be an event is really a construct of a quasi-linguistic system, then one is in a position to undo the construct or to recognize that the construct, by its very nature, has already undone, dismantled, or deconstructed itself — with far-reaching implications for thought of every sort. *Deconstruction* affords a perspective from which any number of modern movements [including political correctness] can be seen as parts of a generalized shift from a logocentric metaphysic of presence to a new recognition of the play of differences among relations. (p. 133-134)

If you find that confusing, consider Barbara Johnson's "clarification" of the term.

Deconstruction is not synonymous with "destruction", however. It is in fact much closer to the original meaning of the word "analysis" itself, which etymologically means "to undo"—a virtual synonym for "to de-construct." The deconstruction of a text does not proceed by random doubt or arbitrary subversion, but by the careful teasing out of warring forces of signification within the text itself. If anything is destroyed in a deconstructive reading, it is not the text, but the claim to unequivocal domination of one mode of signifying over another. A deconstructive reading is a reading which analyses the specificity of a text's critical difference from itself. (*The Critical Difference*, 1981)

Got it? No? Well consider this "elucidation" from J. A. Cuddon's *Dictionary of Literary Terms and Literary Theory.*

Deconstruction owes much to the theories of the French philosopher Jacques Derrida (1930-), whose essay *Structure, Sign , and Play in the Discourse of the Human Sciences* (1966)—which he was to follow with his book *Of Grammatology* (1967)—began a new critical movement. . . . Derrida shows that a text (any text—be it a polemic, a philosophical treatise, a poem, or, for that matter, an exercise in deconstructive criticism) can be read as saying something quite different from what it appears to be saying, and that it may be read as carrying a plurality of significance or as saying many different things which are fundamentally at variance with, contradictory to, and subversive of what may be (or may have been) seen by criticism as a single, stable "meaning . . ." Derrida carries his logic still further to suggest that the language of any discourse is at variance with itself and, by so being, is capable of being read as yet another language. Thus, hypothetically, one may envisage an endless regression of dialectical interpretations and readings without any stable, essential meaning. In short, a text may possess so many different meanings that it cannot have a MEANING. There is no guaranteed essential meaning. (pp. 222-223)

As Professor Dennis points out, "Some scholars actually speak in such arcane and technical language that public understanding of what they do and why they do it is impossible" (*War of Words*, p. 12). The next question is: why would they do this? Professor Dennis suggests that it may well be intentional because "the university is . . . too fearful and too paranoid to really want to have the public know and understand all that occurs on campus" (*War of Words*, p. 12). Perhaps the reason for that is that most universities are funded with public money, and the public just might not stand for some of the nonsense that goes on. So, don't be concerned if you did not understand what you read about deconstruction. In fact, perhaps you should be concerned if you *did* understand what you read. Allow me to attempt to translate, or should I say "deconstruct," but please keep in mind that I am *not* a deconstructionist, I'm not as good at this as others. So let me begin with an academic who would be considered an "authority" on deconstruction. A young man recently visited our campus and gave a talk in the faculty lounge. His presentation was based on his master's thesis, written at East Carolina University, which had recently won the award of the Conference of Southern Deans for the best MA thesis in English. The title of his talk was "Two Kinds of Deconstruction: De Man and Derrida." Paul De Man is Derrida's most famous student/disciple. It might also be noted that De Man was a Nazi, which most scholars agree could account for the anti-semitic strain that seems to run through these PC theories. Nevertheless, the young scholar, who is now a member of the professoriate, referred to Derrida's famous statement, *"Il n'y a pas de texte,"* in his talk and translated that statement as follows: "There is nothing but the text." Now, it just so happens that the Eminent Scholar of the Humanities in our university, Dr. Burton Raffel, was present. (An interview with Professor Raffel appears in chap. 7.) Dr. Raffel is a translator who speaks several languages. When the young deconstructionist's talk was over, Dr. Raffel said, "My friend, I must tell you as a matter of plain, simple fact that you are wrong. *Il n'y a pas de texte'* does not mean, 'There is nothing but the text;' it means 'There is no text' and there is a fundamental difference. Therefore, your entire position is based upon a mistranslation."

Reduced to its simplest terms and taken to its logical conclusion, deconstruction is basically the notion that language is a hopelessly imperfect vehicle for the expression of ideas, and because words have no inherent meaning, "meaning"—*all* meaning—is relative. Words and, as a consequence any piece of writing, can be interpreted in as many different ways as there are people to read them. Make a point about virtually anything, and the deconstructionist will immediately begin nit-picking about the language with which you express your point, rather than addressing the point you raised. Consider the following anecdote.

While sitting in the faculty lounge one day, I expressed

concern over the rising rates of illiteracy in the state of
Louisiana and in the country. One of my colleagues asked
me what "literacy" was. I must admit that my first reaction
was surprise that a professor of English would not know
what the word "literacy" meant. My colleague, however,
was eager to convince me that the word "literacy" could
be defined in so many ways that someone *I* considered to
be "illiterate," based on *my* definition of the word, might
well be more "literate" than I, depending, of course, on
how *that* person defined the term "literacy." In other
words, there was no reason for my concern over literacy
rates because none of us really knew what literacy was
anyway. Get it? Sounds like a politician, doesn't it? Well,
that's politically correct deconstruction, which could be
compared to Orwellian *newspeak* at its best, or would that
be at its worst? Oh well, from a deconstructionist point
of view, it really doesn't matter anyway.

Most English departments offer graduate degrees in
the specific field of rhetoric. While not all rhetoricians are
deconstructionists, rhetoric has become an area in which
one simply cannot avoid "meaningful" contact with
deconstruction and deconstructionists. My department also
allows graduate students to have a rhetoric concentration
at the Ph.D. level. Something called "The Rhetoric Reading
Group" has developed a program to bring together the grad
students and faculty members in the rhetoric program, as
well as any other person in the department who is interested
in this area. Once a month, the group meets at someone's
home for a pot-luck supper and a discussion of an article
in the field of rhetoric which is selected and circulated in
advance.

I hosted the group one evening in my home, and I
invited my next-door neighbor to attend. Now, it just so
happens that my neighbor is also a member of the university
faculty—in the chemistry department. In fact, he is now
the head of that department. He sat quietly listening to the
discussion, which inevitably became an exercise in
deconstruction. For me, such exercises always bring to

mind a line from the movie *Oh God*, when George Burns
says, "You're doing some very funny things with words
here. . . . You've figured out so many ways to talk to each
other that finally nobody can." When my neighbor, the
chemistry professor, was finally asked what he thought,
he simply said, "Please don't tell this stuff to my students."
I suggest that telling a professor of chemistry that words
really have no meaning and that terms really cannot be
defined may not be a good idea. I think the point is, of
course, that while it may be fun for a group of university
faculty members, all of whom have graduate degrees, to
sit around discussing such things, students whose verbal
skills are marginal to begin with would have difficulty
processing such material and need to be more concerned
with learning how to express themselves with clarity.

In addition, I think we must consider the weapon this
theory places in the hands of students of freshman
composition. Instructors who take issue with something
a student writes would have to face the argument that words
have no inherent meaning, which means, of course, that
the instructor could never really understand what the student was trying to say anyway. Ultimately, it becomes
pointless to read or write anything because, according to
deconstruction, no one will ever be able to know what we
were trying to say, nor will we ever be able to know what
anyone else was trying to say.

In other words, aside from the chaos that it naturally
breeds, deconstruction also has the effect of placing all
opinions on an equal footing, particularly when it comes
to reading, understanding, and interpreting writing; and
students today, at least insofar as I have encountered them,
are very quick to attempt to reduce everything to a matter
of opinion, regardless of the topic. I struggle to establish
in the minds of my students that all opinions are *not* created
equal. There are informed opinions and uninformed opinions, educated opinions and uneducated opinions. I point
out that when one is ill, one goes to a medical doctor rather

than a friend, and that is based upon the assumption that the medical doctor's "opinion" is worth more than the average person's, not because the doctor is *better* than anyone else, but because he has studied in the field and knows more about it. Henry H. H. Remak, director of the Institute for Advanced Study at Indiana University, put it eloquently when he said, "In politics a vote is a vote is a vote, but heaven help the university if any opinion is as good as any other opinion provided it is supported by enough vocal self-righteousness" (*Measure*, Nov. 1991, No. 100, p. 2). And the PC crowd is nothing if not self-righteous.

In my opinion, deconstructionist thinking lacks all intellectual discipline because, while I will accept that my students may well define words differently than I, *I* am *paid* to know the definitions of words and to distinguish between writing that is poor, mediocre, good, or excellent. Furthermore, arguing for the notion that the very function of language—i.e., communication of thoughts and ideas— is a self-contradictory proposition, forces us to play mind games rather than attempting to come to a clear understanding of serious issues. As Professor Dennis points out, many if not most of the PC crowd are quite content to play deconstructive mind games like denying the existence and/ or importance of political correctness as a movement, but there are still some who, like Dean Kolodny of the University of Arizona and Professor Berlin of Purdue, are honest enough to admit that their academic careers, both in scholarship and teaching, are merely "extensions" of their "political activism." This was also true in my case.

After completing my Ph.D. in literature at Kansas State University, I took my place among the professoriate. I began my teaching career with the same very liberal ideas and attitudes that I had acquired in the course of my education and that I perceived my colleagues to espouse. I also committed, at least to some extent, the unpardonable sin of presenting my biases as indisputable facts. Pushing attitudes from the professorial pulpit is a knack which involves subtly ridiculing those students who dared to express ideas which were more conservative than those in the party line. The trick was to make it clear without actually saying it that anyone who disagreed with me was immoral or stupid or both. This attitude, of course, is, in the final analysis, antithetical to the very idea of the academy, which, theoretically, is a haven of free speech and a forum for the free and unfettered exchange of information and ideas, whether I agree with those ideas or not.

Unfortunately, this tendency to stifle debate and discussion through ridicule and intimidation is still very widespread on campus. Yet, being politically correct these days means being sensitive enough not to use language which will offend or ridicule (even unintentionally) anyone, and anyone, of course, means gays, lesbians, women, or members of an ethnic minority. But, in the politically correct atmosphere which is prevalent on campus today, if *anyone* happens to be a white male, a fundamentalist Christian, a conservative, a Republican, or any other such politically *in*correct (PNC) individual, belittling them and/ or their views, even to the point of being vicious is not only tolerated, it is encouraged. It is not only always open season on PNC persons, PC persons feel they have a moral obligation to confront and belittle PNC persons as often as they can.

I actually had a student who asked me in class one day if it was possible to be conservative and still be intelligent. The student was genuinely distraught as it is clearly the tendency of many professors, particularly in the humanities (including myself when I first started teaching) to attempt to create the impression that conservatism appeals to the mindless. I informed the student that to be philosophically conservative placed one in the distinguished company of such historical figures as Plato, Edmund Burke, Abraham Lincoln, and Winston Churchill. I also shared with the class Churchill's famous quotation,

"If you are not liberal when you're eighteen, then you have no heart; if you are not conservative when you're thirty, then you have no brain." The student felt better, and so did I.

I consider it the greatest compliment as a teacher when my students have said that they feel comfortable expressing their opinions in my class, even if they know that I disagree with them. Ironically, such compliments have come more frequently *after* I became a conservative convert and an activist in the Republican party. In other words, as I became more politically conservative, I apparently became more intellectually liberal. To understand my point, one must know what I mean when I use the words "liberal" and "conservative," and at the risk of being "politically *in*correct" and offending my deconstructionist colleagues, let me state categorically that words not only *can* be defined, they *must* be defined or we simply cannot communicate with each other. Theories such as deconstructionism involve accepting the sentence of living forever in a huge Tower of Babel. I refuse to accept such a sentence, and I will, therefore, define my terms carefully and thoughtfully and risk the ridicule of the deconstructionists for the sake of clarity.

A colleague of mine, who would classify himself as a liberal, maintains that a liberal is a person who doesn't have the courage to call himself a Communist. Traditionally, a political liberal is one who occupies the left end of the political spectrum. Although the association of liberalism and the Left historically dates back to the physical location of seats in Parliament, a political liberal today is a person who has specific stands on specific issues and a political agenda based upon those stands. For instance, on the issue of abortion, a liberal would be "pro choice," which is a euphemism for being in favor of a woman's right to have an abortion. A political liberal would also have predictable stands on issues like gun control, defense spending, sex education in public schools, prayer in public schools, etc. A political liberal is also a person whose first

reaction to every problem is, "The government should do
something about this." I know this so well because I used
to be one—liberal that is.

A political conservative is one who believes that
government is, at best, a necessary evil and that government
is, at best, inefficient. A political conservative also believes
that anything government can do, individuals and private
enterprise can do better, and anything government does
will take longer and cost more than if it had been done
by individuals or by private enterprise. A political conservative also understands that the liberal reaction to
problems means higher taxes because when the government "does something" about a problem, it inevitably raises
taxes. Like a political liberal, a political conservative has
an agenda based upon his beliefs, and he will have predictable stands on issues like abortion, sex education in
public schools, taxes, etc.

Some political liberals who happen to be college professors are, however, crafty. They know that the word
liberal defined in a non-political, academic sense, is associated with open-mindedness. The word *liberal* in the
phrase *liberal arts*, for instance, means broadly based. This,
of course, is intellectual liberalism, not political liberalism.
But some political liberals who happen to be college
professors either do not recognize or refuse to admit this
critical distinction, and I have heard colleagues of mine
say things like, "I am a liberal because I am open-minded."
This, of course, is a very deceitful play on words, which
presupposes that if one is a political conservative, it is
because one is close-minded.

It is this kind of chicanery which led the media to refer
to the hard-line Communists in the Kremlin as "conservatives" and "right-wingers" in the coverage of the
attempted coup against Mikhail Gorbachev. In fact, any
first-year political science student knows that hard-line
Communists occupy the extreme Left end of the political
spectrum and are, therefore, liberals, not conservatives.

Those old-school Bolsheviks *would* be conservatives in the sense that they were resisting the changes proposed by Gorbachev, but, again, that is not political conservatism; resisting change is intellectual conservatism. In other words, in this case, we have political liberals who are also intellectual conservatives. Still, the media's misleading use of the terms led me to walk into the faculty lounge after the coup in the now defunct Soviet Union and to announce, "Hey, guys, I'm now a left-wing liberal." My colleagues' puzzled expressions led me to explain, "Well, the media says the guys in the Kremlin are 'right-wing conservatives,' so that makes me a 'left-wing liberal.' Get it?"

To clarify, when I say that political correctness (and its attendant "isms," such as multiculturalism, Afrocentrism, genderism, etc.) is "an outgrowth of sixties liberalism and associated with the left in academe. . . ," that means that the proponents of these movements are political liberals who tend to be intellectual conservatives. In other words, most of them have a leftist political agenda, and some of them are among the most close-minded, intolerant individuals I have ever encountered. "What unites them —as firmly as the Christian fundamentalists are united in the belief that the Bible is the revealed Word of God— is their conviction that Western culture and American society are thoroughly racist, sexist, and oppressive" (*New York Magazine*, 21 January 1991, p. 34). A report on race and gender enrichment from Tulane University in 1989, for instance, maintained that, "Racism and sexism are pervasive in America and fundamentally present in all American institutions. . . . Racism and sexism are subtle and, for the most part subconscious or at least subsurface," the report continues, "and it is difficult for us to see and overcome racism because we are all a product of the problem, i.e., we are all the progeny of a racist and sexist society." What this does, of course, is to allow the PC crowd to use hateful epithets like racist and sexist and homophobic to describe anyone who dares to disagree with them, as though these kinds of *ad hominem* attacks settle any and all arguments (see chap. 5).

I wish to state at the outset and in the strongest possible language that I have gone to great lengths to let the PC crowd speak for themselves. I do this because I anticipate that some of the PC crowd will accuse me of distorting their positions and their goals. I choose to address this accusation even before it is made by simply stating that all the statements in this book, which define political correctness and indicate what its agenda is, are quotations from the *proponents* of all the PC "isms." Therefore, if any PC persons attempt to maintain that this book presents a distorted view of their movement and its agenda, the distortion is a result of their own comments.

If you find any of what you are about to read alarming, you need to pay particular attention to the final chapter (chap. 6) entitled "The Road Back to Sanity," because there *are* things that can be done to counteract what I regard as a very dangerous movement in public education. You can also take some comfort in the fact that some things are already being done. For instance, despite the terrorist tactics of the PC crowd on campus to silence the opposition, more and more professors and academicians are speaking out against this movement and its proponents, and it is because of these dissenting voices that there is hope that political correctness (and its attendant isms) will ultimately be exposed as the intellectual fraud that it truly is. While I am proud to add my voice to the dissent, this book will be different from Dinesh D'Souza's *Illiberal Education* in three very important ways.

First of all, Mr. D'Souza writes from the perspective of a student. I, however, write from the perspective of a faculty member who has been teaching in college since 1976, and because I am a college professor with a Ph.D., I have the scholarly credentials to speak against much of the PC nonsense with authority. In other words, I can face the PC professoriate on an equal footing. In addition, I have sat and still sit on committees that are involved in such things as the selection of texts and promotion and tenure matters. This means I have information from my personal experiences that Mr. D'Souza simply could not have access to.

Secondly, I have three children who are now in public schools, one in high school and two in middle school. Furthermore, my wife is a high-school teacher and counselor, and my mother is a vice principal in an elementary school. Therefore, I have personal knowledge of and am in a position to show how this PC movement and all its "innovations" on college campuses have "trickled down" into the secondary and elementary levels and the impact that they have had on instruction at that level.

Finally, I am not interested in engaging in "academy bashing," which is as easy as it is overdone. While I may disagree with the PC crowd on campus, they are still my colleagues and many are my friends. I also think it is necessary to point out that there are quite a few of my colleagues (who are political liberals) who find PC as ridiculous and dangerous as I do. In other words, not all college professors who are political liberals are PC persons; and as Dr. Gary Marotta, Academic Vice-President of my university, points out, "the great number of American academics occupy a rational middle ground."

What I am interested in doing, finally, is arguing *for* the idea of the university as a place for the free and unfettered exchange of ideas and information, for the notion that the job of the scholar is the quest for the truth, *for* the ascendancy of Western culture, *for* the position that higher education must be organized around a canon which includes the "great works" of Western culture, and *for* the notion that history, morality, ethics, decency, truth, and discipline are neither dirty words nor merely matters of opinion. These positions, of course, make me very politically *in*correct (PNC).

Chapter 2

MULTICULTURALISM

The politically correct movement has manifested itself in a variety of ways on college campuses across the country, not the least of which is in the trend that has come to be known as "multiculturalism" (MC). Though the link between political correctness and multiculturalism has been questioned, there is more than enough evidence to indicate that these two things are intimately connected. Again, the very name of the conference at Berkeley mentioned in chapter 1, "Political Correctness and Cultural Studies," is a clear indication that "multiculturalism" and "political correctness" are indeed very closely related. As already mentioned, Professor Dennis of Columbia University maintains that political correctness and multiculturalism are "conceptual companion[s] in the campus debate." He even points out that "political correctness is sometimes regarded as the enforcement arm of multiculturalism" (*War of Words*, p. 7).

Professor Dennis also points out, I think correctly, that "for a time, multicultural concerns were hardly controversial" (*War of Words*, p. 5). When I first encountered multiculturalism, it seemed innocuous enough. Its stated purpose is to "expand the canon of traditional studies," specifically in the humanities, to include the experiences of the ethnic minorities which compose a significant part of the population of the United States today. Okay, I thought, no big deal. In fact, I again agree with Professor Dennis when he says that "in principle, [the goals] are rather noble." After all, America is the land of "*e pluribus unum*," and the notion that American society is a patchwork of many races and cultures seemed to me nothing more than a penetrating glimpse into the obvious. Insofar as multiculturalism advocates that we should respect all cultures (to the extent to which they deserve respect) and that we should broaden our own world view by considering other cultural perspectives, I not only do not have a problem with it, I support it. But, alas, when multiculturalism becomes PC, there is much more to it, and that is when my objection and opposition begin.

One area in which the impact of politically correct multiculturalism (PC/MC) can be observed is in the proliferation of specialized courses some of which have become programs of study some of which have become departments which now offer degrees in areas like Chicano studies, African-American studies (see chap. 3), women's studies, and gay and lesbian studies (see chap. 4). As this trend continues, battles over academic turf are inevitable. The *Chronicle of Higher Education* has reported on several such confrontations which have already occurred at universities across the country (see chap. 5).

The move toward PC/MC (or "diversity" as some have called it) has also manifested itself in the attempt to redefine traditional courses of study, and courses in freshman composition have become one of the main focal points of this effort. I believe that there are two reasons for this. First, all students on campus must take these courses. Secondly, unlike freshman math courses (the only other courses all students must take), the content of freshman comp classes tends to be more fluid and less rigidly defined. Because the focus of these courses is writing, the topics are generally open, which leaves a certain latitude in the selection of material that will be presented.

Consider the following titles and their publishers: *Visions Across the Americas,* Harcourt, Brace, and Jovanovich; *Our Times, Ourselves Among Others*, and *Rereading America: Cultural Contexts for Critical Thinking and Writing* St. Martin Press; *Encountering Cultures*, Prentice-Hall; *One World, Many Cultures*, MacMillan;

American Mosaic: Multicultural Readings in Context,
Houghton-Miflin; *Cultural Tapestry: Readings for a*
Pluralistic Society, Harper-Collins. These are *all* textbooks intended for use as readers in freshman composition
courses.

The reason I am aware of these titles is because
complimentary copies of these books were sent to me by
the publishers. I was selected to receive these books
because I sit on the Freshman Committee of the English
Department at my university, which is the committee
which is responsible for selecting texts for the freshman
composition program. The aforementioned books are all
offered by major publishing houses with national distribution, and such publishing houses do not even print texts
until they have marketing analyses that indicate clear and
widespread demand. The titles of the texts mentioned offer
indisputable evidence that freshman composition programs
have, indeed, become the focus of the demand for
multicultural approaches to traditional courses on college
campuses, and the size of the publishing houses offering
these texts is proof of how widespread that demand
is. Consider the following examples.

In 1989, black students at Wooster College staged a
sit-in, demanding a black-studies requirement at that college. The "compromise" which was reached with the
students was a three year commitment to change the focus
of the required freshman seminar. As a result, for the past
two years, the title of the required freshman seminar at
Wooster College has been "Difference, Power, Discrimination: Perspectives on Race, Gender, Class, and Culture."
According to the *Chronicle of Higher Education,* the
course is meant to teach the campus' 480 freshmen to think
and write critically and "has focused on racism and sexism
in the American Society" (p. A-33).

In the interest of fairness, it should be noted that the
Chronicle reported that "most freshmen say they find the
course stimulating and useful;" however, "some older

students worry that the seminar, and a related speaker series, establishes a one-sided conversation about political issues on campus" (p. A-33). Others have gone even farther and "call the seminar a lopsided, left-wing attempt to reduce American culture to victims and victimizers. White men especially say they are too often made the bad guys" (p. A-35).

The seminar was covered for the student newspaper by Jeremiah Jenne who said the course "fell short of its goals by aggravating conservatives and soothing liberals without creating a useful dialogue between them." The editor of the student newspaper, *The Wooster Voice*, Mark Osgoode Smith, says that the seminar's "messages get twisted as they drift further into the undergraduate culture."

Jeremiah Jenne also said the "lecture series is heavily weighted with liberal speakers" (p. A-35). It was also reported that when former New York City Mayor Ed Koch spoke at Wooster and criticized affirmative action, he received "a hostile reaction." Lynne V. Chenney, chair of the National Endowment for the Humanities, in a September speech recounted a former Wooster student's description of the college as "an intolerant re-education camp" (p. A-35). Smith adds that "students feel more oppressed by the political climate the more time they spend at Wooster" (p. A-35). In December of 1991, Douglas L. Miller, a sophomore at Wooster, "announced in the student newspaper that he was leaving the college because of the political climate on the campus," calling the college "a vast laboratory of brainwashing" (p. A-33).

The 19 December 1990 issue of the *Chronicle of Higher Education* contains a story on two freshman writing courses at the University of Massachusetts at Amherst which have been "revamped . . . so all the readings raise issues of race and social diversity. Since most freshmen are required to take writing, the faculty reasoned, they [the students] would have to deal with those issues." The two courses are Basic Writing and College Writing. The students enrolled in Basic Writing "are required to read and discuss literature in which characters routinely experience some kind of discrimination," while students "in the more advanced College Writing work with materials from periodical and broadcast media that raise issues of diversity" (*Chronicle*, 19 December 1990, p. A-13). Marcia S. Curtis, the assistant director of the writing program at the U. of Mass. at Amherst and the person in charge of the task of compiling the reading list for the "revamped freshman composition courses," said that she specifically did "not want the old canon that is all white, mostly male, and European centered" (p. A-14).

It seems "the writing faculty, along with faculties in other disciplines, agreed that something had to be done to educate Amherst's predominantly white students about racism." So, the Amherst composition faculty decided "to integrate multicultural awareness into freshman composition . . . to provide 'prompts' that encourage students to reflect on their own experiences and deal with their own prejudices" (p. A-13). Apparently, it was felt that this was also necessary for the faculty, so "sensitivity workshops" are also now part of the writing program at the U. of Mass. at Amherst and are "required for the forty or so new teaching assistants who join the program each year and for faculty members from the English Department who take turns teaching freshman composition" (p. A-14). Anne J. Herrington, associate professor of English and director of the writing program at Amherst, says, "Keeping the focus of freshman composition on racial and social diversity requires continuous vigilance" (p. A-14). Obviously, Professor Herrington's statement makes it quite clear that the new focus is not accidental, and the U. of Mass. at Amherst is not the only example of such a conscious move in English departments.

A series of articles in the *Chronicle* told the story of a similar move at the University of Texas at Austin. In

May of 1990 "an English Department Committee . . . prepared a revised syllabus for a freshman writing course [English 306] that focused on the theme of 'difference.'" The course, "officially called 'Writing About Difference'," had, according to Joseph Horn, a professor of psychology at U. T. at Austin, "a strongly political message" (*Chronicle*, 21 November 1990, p. A-15).

In fact, critics of the course began calling it "Oppression English" and "a thinly veiled attempt at political indoctrination. Students, they argued, would feel pressured to conform to 'politically correct' views on such issues as sexual discrimination and affirmative action, and would devote more time to learning about oppression than they would about correct sentence structures." The critics of the course also contended that "the proposed readings were consistently leftist" (*Chronicle*, 21 November 1990, p. A-15). The Fall 1990 newsletter of the National Association of Scholars, based at Princeton, called the move at U. T. "a not-so-subtle attempt to convert a required course into what could be called a 'mass consciousness-raising seminar in racism and sexism.'" Ultimately, a "Statement of Concern" was circulated and signed by fifty-six faculty members, and "the deans of at least three other colleges have also expressed doubts about the course, and at least one other is said to be considering a substitute course" (*Chronicle*, 20 February 1991, p. A-18).

The supporters of the course (the PC crowd) then began talking of "a right-wing conspiracy" and "academic death squads." It was also charged that it was arranged for critics of the course to be "harangued by name during campus rallies, ostracized by their colleagues, and characterized as racist and sexist" (*Chronicle*, 21 November 1990, p. A-15). As already mentioned, this is a typical tactic of the PC crowd.

The conclusion of the story is that the English Department at U. T. at Austin approved the course in September of 1991 by a vote of 46 to 11. Final approval, which will have to come from the dean of the College of Liberal Arts, Standish Meacham, and the president of the university, William H. Cunningham, is expected before the end of the 1991-92 academic year. This reveals not only the presence of political correctness / multiculturalism, but the strength of its influence.

The controversy caused by this course in freshman composition at U. T. at Austin "reflects the contentious debates taking place nationwide over whether, and how, curricula should be revised to promote awareness of cultural diversity" (*Chronicle,* 21 November 1990, p. A-15). And, as is usually the case with such "innovations," the debate has "trickled down" into the elementary and secondary school systems. It has manifested itself in several areas, not the least of which has been the controversy over "bilingual" programs. At first glance, one might assume that "bilingual" education would involve students studying other languages as part of their educational experience, which, of course, would not be a problem. Unfortunately, such is not the case. The demand for "bilingual" education is the demand that students from other cultures be taught regular academic subjects in their "native" language and be allowed to study English as a second language.

Opponents of such moves, of which I am one, take the position that, for anyone who lives in the United States, English *is* their "native" language. I further maintain that, like it or not, English is the language of the marketplace, domestically *and* internationally, and students in this country who are allowed to go through school without becoming proficient in English will find themselves at a serious economic disadvantage when they graduate. This, of course, is a very politically *in*correct position, but I like living on the edge.

There have also been demands that black students be allowed to write in "black English." My position on that (speaking of living on the edge) has been that "black

English" is a dialect and students do not have to come to school to learn to be proficient in a dialect. Students come to school to learn to be proficient in *standard* English. Again, standard English is the language of the marketplace, and proficiency in that language provides economic advantages. This position, too, is very politically *in*correct, and many in academe abandoned standard approaches to teaching standard English long ago.

The year I began teaching (1976), I was enrolled in a course required for all graduate teaching assistants at the university called English 590—The Teaching of Remedial English. The professor who was teaching the class had just published a textbook on the subject of teaching "remedial" writing. His position was that we (educators) had been teaching grammar and making our students diagram sentences for years, and they still had not learned to write. So we stopped teaching grammar and we stopped diagramming sentences more than ten or fifteen years ago, and that was long before the phrase "politically correct" was ever used.

Another example of the move toward politically correct multicultural approaches to traditional courses at the university level is the tendency to attack the "canon." The canon is a body of "great books" produced by "great writers," which was supposed to include what Matthew Arnold called "the best that has been thought and written." You could expect to find on this list such writers as Homer, Plato, Aristotle, Virgil, Chaucer, Shakespeare, Dante, Milton, Wordsworth, Twain, etc. The politically correct position on the canon today was articulated by Stanley Hauerwas, a professor at the Divinity School at Duke, who said, "The canon of great literature was created by high-Anglican a—h—— to underwrite their social class." In other words, the "great books" of Western civilization are now regarded by politically correct academicians merely as "a propaganda exercise to reinforce the notion of white-male superiority" (*New York Magazine*, 21 January 1991, p. 36).

Such movements are quite common on college campuses across the country today, and Linda Gordon, professor of history at the University of Wisconsin at Madison maintains that it is "conservative academics who . . . oppose expanding the traditional canon of literary texts and historical topics to include material on previously excluded groups" (*Chronicle*, 16 January 1991, p. A-6). Speaking as one of those "conservative academics" to whom Professor Gordon refers, let me state flatly that her statement is simply not true. I have encountered no opposition whatsoever to "expanding the traditional canon," but there is serious opposition to doing away with a canon altogether, which is and has been the real agenda of the PC/MC crowd for more than twenty years.

The PC crowd has also taken the position that it is impossible to establish a "canon" because you could never get agreement as to what should be included. I served on a committee of university professors and high-school teachers that attempted to establish a list of books which kids *should* have read by the time they graduated from high school. We circulated a questionnaire among the English department faculty at U.S.L. asking for titles for the list. After compiling the titles and eliminating repetition, we came up with a list which, with only slight variations, was remarkably similar to all other such lists that have ever been produced. So, the notion that there is not enough of a consensus among academics to create a "canon" is also not true.

A specific example of the PC/MC movement to eliminate the canon can be found at the University of Arizona where a new series of humanities courses entitled "Critical Concepts in Western Culture" is now being offered. In this series of courses "students are examining ideas associated with Western civilization, but they're looking at them from various cultural perspectives" (*Chronicle*, 29 May 1991, p. A-9). J. Douglas Canfield, a professor of comparative literature at Arizona and the man who developed the first two courses in the series, says, "We developed the sequence as an alternative to the traditional, canonical 'great books' course. We wanted to better understand and critique Western texts by placing them in juxtaposition to popular and non-western culture" (*Chronicle*, 29 May 1991, p. A-9). The key word in Professor Canfield's description of the courses is "alternative," which clearly indicates that this movement has gone beyond merely *expanding* the canon (to which no genuine scholar would object) to revising it completely.

There is, however, a problem here because of two very simple facts. The first fact is that before you can "better understand and critique Western texts by placing them in juxtaposition to popular and non-western culture," which is the stated goal of the University of Arizona's new series of courses in the humanities, you must first have students who *know* the "great works" of Western civilization. The second fact is, unfortunately, many if not most of our students today are not only *not* familiar with the "great works" of Western civilization, they are not familiar with Western civilization. And, not only are they unfamiliar with the history of Western civilization, they also know very little about the history of their own country. But history, itself, is yet another victim of the politically correct move toward multiculturalism.

When asked by a deconstructionist colleague to define "history," my response was, "History is the chronology of important events in the saga of humanity." Then came the inevitable response. "Ah, but what is *important?*" I conceded my colleague's point that the word, "important," may, indeed, have different meanings for different people. But when it comes to history, I asserted my belief that the "importance" of an event is relative to the number of people affected by that event. For instance, the death of any individual is tragic, for as John Donne said, "Any man's death diminishes me, because I am involved in mankind; and therefore never send to know for whom the bell tolls; it tolls for thee." Donne, of course, was very politically incorrect for his generic use of the words "man" and "mankind" to mean all people (see chap. 4). Nevertheless, his sentiment, I think, is valid. But while the death of any individual is tragic, the deaths of, for instance, heads of state are recorded in history books because their lives affected so many more people than the average person. To be specific, the death of Abraham Lincoln was more "important" in the ultimate scheme of human history than the death of a particular friend of mine who died at a very young age. Even though my friend's passing shall always be recorded in my heart and mind, no history book shall bear his name, and I do not bear history a grudge for that fact.

My PC colleagues, however, would press on for, remember, according to deconstruction, "the concept of thing, substance, event, and absolute recedes, to be superseded by the concept of relation, ratio, and relativity." In other words, when is an event an event? According to a deconstructive approach to history, *never!* Will we ever know, for instance, the exact causes of the First World War? My PC colleagues would point out that the causes were as many as they were complex and that historians are still not in total agreement as to exactly how and why the First World War happened. Again, while I would concede that point, I would also argue that there is *absolute* agreement that there *was* a First World War and that it was a very "important" historical event. Along the same lines, we may never know the *whole* story of the assassination of John Kennedy, but we do know that he was assassinated and that this, too, was an "important" historical event.

If my thinking makes sense to you, then you are, like me, very politically incorrect. The position being pushed from the politically correct professoriate is that history is no longer and never was "definitive." The idea that history is "a non-biased and accurate reflection of the past . . . is now being shattered by . . . current theories that knowl-

edge is subjective." Peter Novick, a professor of history
at the University of Chicago, wrote and published in 1988
a book entitled *That Noble Dream: The "Objectivity Question" and the American Historical Profession.* The book
challenges "the commitment to objectivity" as "the central
norm of the profession [of historians]." "We should disregard far-reaching claims to objectivity," Professor Novick
proclaims. "We don't have to be definitive," he says; "we
can just be interesting or suggestive." He further maintains
that "the 1960's ushered in 'the present period of confusion, polarization, and uncertainty, in which the idea of
historical objectivity has become more problematic than
ever before'" (*Chronicle*, 16 January 1991, p. A-4).

Linda Gordon, professor of history at the University
of Wisconsin at Madison, echoes Mr. Novick's position
and maintains that "the most interesting debates in scholarship today are not at heart about objectivity and the
nature of historical knowledge, but about politics. Political
agendas," she continues, "are the real determinants of
different approaches to writing history today." (*Chronicle*,
16 January 1991, p. A-5). In other words, it is a very short
step from challenging the "objectivity" of history to
defending and even advocating using history to suit a
"political agenda," a step which has clearly been taken
by the PC / MC crowd on college campuses. The problem
is that when one is using history in such a manner, distortions of the facts, even to the point of lying, never seems
too far away. This is exactly what Joseph Stalin did in
the Soviet Union when consolidating his power.

To be sure, this movement has its critics. There is
serious opposition to abandoning the rigid, scholarly
standards to which all professors in the humanities have
traditionally been held for the sake of being "interesting
and suggestive" or for the sake of "political agendas,"
which is the stated direction of the PC/MC movement. One
such critic is Dr. Gary Marotta (see chap. 7). In an interview
with me, Dr. Marotta stated, "Those who advocate such
positions are the historical equivalents of literary critics

who subscribe to deconstructionism. They say, 'There is no truth' and, 'We can never know truth wholly.' . . . We must believe in truth, and we must believe in objectivity even though we know we cannot fully describe it or fully achieve it. To say there is none, then that gives merit to the notion that everything can be manipulated." Another critic of "new history" is Gertrude Himmelfarb, professor emeritus at the Graduate School of the City University of New York.

Professor Himmelfarb, considered one of the leading historians of Victorian England, delivered the 20th annual Jefferson Lecture sponsored by the National Endowment for the Humanities. The invitation to give this lecture is the highest honor conferred by the U. S. government in recognition of outstanding achievement in the humanities. Professor Himmelfarb is a "vehement critic of most of the newer approaches that have taken root in the discipline in the last 20 or 30 years," and in her lecture, she "assail[ed] what she sees as the failings of the 'new history'—by which she means social history, psychoanalytical history, quantitative history, structuralist history, and, indeed, just about any other kind that is not traditional political history" (*Chronicle*, 1 May 1991, p. A-4). She defines traditional history "as a chronological narrative of significant political events. . . . 'History is defined by its narrative, primarily,' she said, 'and without that narrative there would be no structure for history. That narrative is basically composed of major political events . . . great men and great events and great ideas have always been, and should remain, the 'heart of history.'" She added that traditional history "doesn't decide in advance what the pattern of history is going to be for all times and all places. And in a sense these new modes of history do that." Professor Himmelfarb also "expressed concern, in particular, about the recent generation of graduate students who, she said, have been taught nothing but the new history and are discouraged from pursuing anything else" (*Chronicle*, 1 May 1991, p. A-8).

Diane Ravitch, a professor of history of education at Columbia University, and Pulitzer Prize winner Arthur Schlesinger, Jr. ". . . say they fear many scholars don't understand the extent to which many existing curricula are already multicultural." According to the *Chronicle of Higher Education,* "a growing number of school districts, such as those in Washington and in Prince George's County in Maryland, are committing themselves to infusing a multicultural perspective into their curricula," and Schlesinger warns that, in the wake of the move to multiculturalism, "the metaphor of America as a melting pot . . . is giving way to a Tower of Babel," and that "many historians underestimate the threat posed . . . to principles of sound scholarship and to social cohesiveness" (*Chronicle,* 6 February 1991, p. A-7).

None of these arguments, however, have stopped the politically correct move toward multicultural approaches to education and the "deconstruction" of history, and, as with composition, this is not just happening at the university level. Professor Ali Masri of the University of New York, who also appeared on ABC's "Nightline," maintained that, "Schools are killers of cultures. Minority cultures are destroyed by schools." In keeping with this new thinking and spirit, the executive board of the Organization of American Historians recently issued a statement asserting the importance of studying race, class, sex, and ethnicity in history classes in public schools. Gary B. Nash, a member of the organization's board and a professor of history at the University of California at Los Angeles, calls the statement "a strong endorsement of multiculturalism." Terrie L. Epstein, professor of education at Boston College, calls the opposition to multiculturalism "conservative" and maintains that "most public school teachers are more liberal." Professor Epstein further contends that public school teachers "have already made the decision to incorporate multiculturalism into their classrooms and are merely looking for guidance and materials to do so" (*Chronicle*, 6 February 1991, p. A-5).

In response to this search for "guidance and materials," The New York State Board of Regents convened a Task Force on Minorities. This task force was set up by Commissioner Thomas Sobol with the purpose of ". . . purging the state's curriculum of 'Euro-centrism'" (*The Boston Herald*, 19 August 1991, p. 23). The chief consultant to this task force, called "the group's guru" by the *Boston Herald*, was none other than Leonard Jefferies, chair of the Department of Black Studies at City University of New York. There will be much more on Professor Jefferies in the next chapter.

The task force prepared a report entitled "One Nation, Many Peoples" (*very* PC) and submitted it to the Board. The report proclaimed that, "Intellectual and educational oppression . . . has characterized the culture and institutions of the United States and the European American world for centuries" (*New York Magazine*, 21 January 1991, p. 34). Among other things, the report suggested that "all curricular materials [including those in math and science] be prepared on the basis of multicultural contributions." The result would be that "children from minority cultures will have higher self-esteem and self-respect, while children from European cultures will have a less arrogant perspective" (*New York Magazine*, p. 40). The report also calls the U. S. Constitution "the embodiment of the White Male with Property Model" (*New York Magazine*, p. 35).

Lawrence Auster, a free-lance writer who was on hand at the meeting when the report was submitted, was offended by what he called "the Regents' failure to engage in a substantive debate on an issue which had occasioned so much controversy" (*Measure*, Nov. 1991, No. 100, p. 1). According to Auster, "There was no disagreement with the report's central idea of de-emphasizing historical knowledge and replacing it with the technique of looking at the world through 'multiple perspectives' "

(*Measure*, p. 3). Auster also concluded after sitting through the meeting that "multiculturalism has become the status quo" (*Measure*, p. 3). Chancellor Emeritus Willard Genrich declared that, "The present syllabus [for the state of New York] is already multiculturalist, starting in kindergarten, with constant emphasis on understanding different cultures." Commissioner J. Edward Meyer stated, "We have multicultural plans going back to 1980." Chancellor Martin Barell maintained, "When I was in school, we didn't learn about slavery, we didn't learn about pushing back the Indians. This curriculum is just about telling the truth" (*Measure*, p.3). Commissioner Shirley Brown added, "How can anyone object to including more fairness and telling more of the truth?" (*Measure*, p. 4).

Auster observed that the "truth" the curriculum is "telling" ". . . has nothing to do with knowledge as it is normally understood, but with the contemporary version of 'morality,' . . . " and that ". . . the emphasis on 'moral perspectives' also places in an even more alarming light the proposal to downplay historical information." The rhetoric of the Commission "consisted of emotionally laden references to blacks' historical second-class citizenship, echoing the implicit notion that multiculturalism is on the same moral plane as the abolition of slavery" (*Measure*, p. 3). This, of course, is right in line with the politically correct assumption that history is "not about objectivity" but about "political agendas" and that history "can be interesting and suggestive" rather than "definitive." Finally, after sitting through the entire meeting, Auster concluded that, as far as the New York Regents were concerned, "multiculturalism is not about 'understanding different cultures,' as it claims, but about pushing an alienated view of American culture and history." The "discussion" held by the New York Board of Education "made it clear," according to Auster, that "an 'adequate' curriculum was defined by the Regents as one which showed 'enough' shameful things about our past" (*Mea-*

sure, p. 4). Auster even quoted one commissioner as saying, "We don't need textbooks on World War II. We only need to ask one question: Why was the bomb dropped?" (*Measure*, p. 3).

But, perhaps the most serious problem with the move toward multiculturalism was pointed out by a New York City social studies teacher, ironically an immigrant from India, when she said, "We're trying to teach global culture to ninth graders who have no idea of their own country. I feel they should be well grounded in American history and then integrate the larger knowledge of the world into that'" (*Measure*, p. 1). In the state of New York, "the 1987 curriculum includes, *inter alia* [among other things], a two-year sequence on Global Cultures in ninth and tenth grade which gives 'equal time' to all the continents. American history is not studied until 11th grade" (*Measure*, p. 1).

The New York Board of Regents' report led "a group of prominent historians—including several past presidents of prestigious scholarly associations—[to] issue a widely publicized statement that attacked [the] New York State curriculum report [One Nation, Many Peoples] for 'ethnic cheerleading' and for violating 'commonly accepted standards of evidence' in the study of history" (*Chronicle*, 6 February 1991, p. A-6). Still, the New York State Board of Regents adopted the report and all its recommendations with only three dissenting votes. Pat Geyer would have applauded.

Patricia Geyer, who recently appeared on an ABC "Nightline" program devoted entirely to the impact of PC on history instruction, proudly admitted that she "teaches history differently now than she used to ten years ago." A schoolteacher for twenty-five years, Ms. Geyer is presently teaching world history and economics at the West Campus of Sacramento's Johnson High School. She stated that the reason she teaches differently now is that her "clientele has changed." Ms. Geyer also maintained

that, "History is what is important to you." Now that's
an interesting position. I wondered how a master's committee would react if when it came time for a graduate
student in history to take his or her generals, that student
said to the committee, "Now you can only test me on what's
important to me." Well, I guess one could try it.

Ms. Geyer also said that she has changed the way she
teaches World War II because she now has Oriental students in her class. "When we talked about World War II,"
she said, "we gave the official story. . . . *Now* I have to
say, 'How did the Japanese feel about this? Why did they
do these things? What were their reasons?'" Another guest
on the show, Manning Marable, a professor at the Center
for the Study of Ethnicity and Race in America at the
University of Colorado, agreed with Ms. Geyer and said,
"When we talk about the history of the Second World War,
very infrequently is it mentioned that nearly one hundred
thousand Japanese-Americans were denied their constitutional rights and placed in internment camps."

I would suggest that there are four problems with
Professor Marable's observation. First of all, speaking of
telling the whole story, the internment of Japanese-Americans was done by liberal Democrat Franklin D. Roosevelt,
but Professor Marable failed to mention that. I wonder
why? Secondly, the Japanese-Americans received resti-
tution for that internment. He didn't mention that either.
Thirdly, what is more important in understanding the
history of that period: the internment of Japanese-Americans or the unspeakable horrors of German and Japanese
aggression?

I suggest that a clear understanding of history rests
on both a knowledge of the facts *and* an accurate perspective on the relative "importance" of those facts. And the
deconstructionists can go to the devil! The bombing of
Pearl Harbor is more significant in the history of that period
than the internment of Japanese-Americans. And if one
considers the nature of the Nazi internment camps, those

in this country really *are* hardly worth mentioning, unless Professor Marable is prepared to argue that there is no substantive difference between the camps in this country and Auschwitz.

This is *not* to say that the internment of Japanese-Americans shouldn't be mentioned; it should, but these new approaches to history tend to focus on historical minutiae to the point of distorting the overall picture, which is the fourth problem I have with Professor Marable's position. As in photography, if one focuses on an object in the background or on the periphery, the resulting picture will be out of focus. As a case in point, former Education Secretary William Bennett, who appeared on that same program, said, "I saw in the context of the Pearl Harbor discussion [during the 50th anniversary of the bombing] a group of students who were talking about Pearl Harbor and World War II, and one of them said, 'Well, I understand our conduct during that war was racist, but at least it wasn't sexist.'"

My response is how dare any teacher leave the impression in the mind of even one student that the behavior of the United States in World War II was "racist." Yet, this is exactly the result of what Bennett called "the new attitudinizing" about history that PC multiculturalism has led to. And to answer the question raised by one of the members of the New York Board of Regents, the bomb was dropped because the Japanese would not surrender, and taking out the Japanese military one island at a time, and ultimately one house at a time when we got to the mainland, would have cost hundreds of thousands of additional American *and* Japanese lives, and I say "Give 'em hell, Harry!" And furthermore, if the person who asked this question really didn't know the answer to it, I would say that person is not qualified to be a high-ranking official in the educational bureaucracy in this country.

Another manifestation of PC multiculturalism is the vilification of Christopher Columbus. Berkeley,

California changed the name of its Columbus Day celebration to "Indigenous Peoples Day." Columbus has become something on the order of the anti-Christ to the PC multiculturalists obviously because he is the carrier of a "cultural plague," the one who brought the "filthy," white, European, male-dominated system to this "pristine" continent. What is now completely left out of the discussions I have heard concerning Columbus' proper place in history is that when Columbus embarked on his historic journey in 1492, most people still believed that the earth was flat and that ships that ventured too far out would fall off the edge. I would suggest that, in such an atmosphere, it took some degree of vision and courage even to attempt such a voyage. But alas, in the wonderful world of PC, white European males are transgressors and oppressors and villains who are not capable of possessing things like vision and courage.

So what is the end result of all these "innovations" in our system of public education? In January of 1992, President George Bush visited Japan. Accompanying him were the chief executives of the three major automobile manufacturers who spent most of the trip complaining about the Japanese not buying their products. Japan's first response was that American manufacturers must first make something that the Japanese want to buy. After the president and his entourage left, the Speaker of the Japanese Parliament called America "a Japanese subcontractor." The Speaker also said that American workers are "lazy, overpaid, and illiterate." One week later, another high-ranking member of the Japanese government said that America's executives were also "inferior." Immediately, Japan-bashing came into vogue, but I have never been fond of the "kill-the-messenger" syndrome. I have always believed that if someone speaks the truth, then what that person is saying is important, whether I like it or not. The important question then is, "Were the Japanese officials speaking the truth?"

When I served as a delegate-at-large to the 1988 Republican National Convention in New Orleans, I was invited to attend a seminar entitled *Excellence in Education.* The seminar was sponsored by the McDonnell-Douglas Corp., and the panel included William J. Bennett, the Secretary of Education; Robert D. Orr, governor of Indiana; William Brock, former Secretary of Labor; and Terrel H. Bell, former Secretary of Education.

The Secretaries were armed with fresh statistics from recent international academic competitions in which, to put it mildly, the United States got its ears boxed. With seventeen countries participating, U.S. students finished thirteenth in physics, fifteenth in chemistry, and dead last in biology. Countries which outpaced us included Czechoslovakia, Poland, and Mexico.

Albert Shanker, president of the American Federation of Teachers, pointed out that the International Association for the Evaluation of Educational Achievement (IEA) did some interesting analyses. The country with the highest scores in the fourteen-year-old category was Hungary. IEA determined the percentage of schools in the other participating countries which scored lower than Hungary's worst school. Only 1 percent of Swedish and Japanese schools and 5 percent of Korean schools performed at a level that was lower than Hungary's worst. 16 percent of Dutch schools and 19 percent of British schools fell below the mark of Hungary's worst. Get ready. Of U.S. schools, 30 percent, almost one third, achieved lower scores than Hungary's worst schools. Only Italian schools compared more poorly than ours.

When considering individual students, data revealed that the *average* student in Japan outperformed the top 1 percent of our students in the sciences and that the *worst* students from Hong Kong out performed 98 percent of our kids. Only students from the Philippines had a lower average score than our kids. What is even more discouraging is that U.S. students with the lowest scores were performing at a level which was only slightly above chance. In other words, if our worst students *had simply filled in* answer sheets randomly without even reading the questions, they would have done only slightly worse. In similar competitions conducted in 1991 with fourteen countries participating, the U.S. finished 12th in math and 13th in science.

This data clearly establishes that the United States is one of the least-successful developed, industrialized nations in the world when it comes to its efforts to educate its young people. According to "ABC News," only 7 percent of our high-school graduates are adequately prepared to study science at the college level, and three out of four high-school graduates lack the math skills to compete or even function in today's high-tech world. In the same program on ABC, results of a test administered to high-school students across the country by the National Assessment of Academic Progress were given. Here are samples of the questions on the test, and following the questions are the percentage of students who answered correctly. Please keep in mind that these were multiple choice questions, so the correct answers were in front of the students; they simply had to identify them.

In the area of history:

(1) What brought the U. S. into World War II? 81 percent (2) What is the Constitutional concept that separates powers among the three branches of government? 64 percent (3) What did the Monroe Doctrine declare? 42 percent (4) What was Brown vs. Board of Education? 22 percent

In the area of literature:

(1) What F. Scott Fitzgerald novel is about wealth in America? 69 percent (2) Who said, "A penny saved is a penny earned"? 42 percent (3) What is *The Grapes of Wrath* about? 38 percent (4) What is *1984* about? 25 percent

In the area of math and science:

(1) 87% of 10—Is the answer greater than, less than, or equal to 10? 60 percent (2) You have ten coins. One is a quarter; one is a nickel; one is a penny. What is the *least* amount of money you could have? 38 percent (3) Why does algae grow on top of the water? 51 percent

The national averages on the test were as follows: History—54 percent; Literature—52 percent; Math—63 percent; Science—55 percent. In other words, failing in every category. On the same program, ABC asked kids across the country some current events questions, just to see what they actually did know. The nuclear accident at Chernoble was in the news at the time, so the kids were asked what Chernoble was. Among the responses ABC got was that Chernoble was Cher's full name.

Along the same lines, Gallup did a study to find out what young adults knew about geography. The results were published in *U. S. News & World Report*, and our kids came in last, behind the groups from West Germany, Sweden, Italy, France, Britain, Canada, Japan, and Mexico. Consider this: among Americans age eighteen to twenty four, given a blank world map, 20 percent could not properly identify the United States of America; 22 percent could not pick out Canada; 26 percent could not identify Mexico; 32 percent could not find the Pacific Ocean; 60 percent did not know where Central America was; 63 percent could not identify France; 70 percent could not find England.

Gallup's first study in this area was conducted in 1947, and at that time, 60 percent of that same age group knew where Spain was; now only 32 percent know. These facts tell us one of two things. Either American kids are twice as stupid today as they were in 1947, or they are not being taught what they once were taught. I suggest the latter is obviously the case, and it is the education establishment in this country which is responsible. It was in the 1960s that we started taking new and "enlightened" approaches to education in this country and began teaching something

called "Social Living" instead of geography. The result
is that our kids no longer know where anything is or much
of anything else.

In August of 1990, the *Morning Advocate*, a newspaper in Baton Rouge, Louisiana, reported that the College
Board, a private, non-profit membership organization based
in New York representing over twenty-seven-hundred
colleges, universities, secondary schools, and other educational associations, announced that scores on the Scholastic Aptitude Test (SAT), which students take to enter
college, had dropped for the third consecutive year and
that verbal scores had sunk to a ten-year low. College board
president Donald M. Stewart was quoted in that article
as saying, "Reading is in danger of becoming a lost art
among many American students—and that would be a
national tragedy." As if to confirm President Stewart's
grim prediction, according to an article published in the
Boston Herald in September of 1991, verbal scores on the
SAT plummeted again last year to a new *twenty* -year low.

So it appears that we have also stopped teaching
reading along with traditional history and geography and
that reading is, indeed, "in danger of becoming a lost art
among many American students." The *Advocate* article
goes on to state that these "scores and the stagnation in
student achievement that they suggest will almost certainly
fuel public doubts about the success of the decade-old
school reform movement." I would take issue only with
the phrase "decade-old;" the movement is much older than
that. In fact, as I have already suggested, it began in the
1960s.

In July of 1990, the Associated Press ran a story out
of its Washington bureau that featured the results of a
survey taken by the National Alliance of Business (NAB).
The survey found that "64 percent of major U. S.
companies are not happy with the reading, writing, and
reasoning abilities of high-school graduates entering the
work force," and that "72 percent of executives polled also

thought new employees' math skills had worsened." NAB president William Kolberg, a former assistant Secretary of Labor and administrator of the Employment and Training Administration from 1973-77, warned, "We are on a collision course with the reality that America is developing a second-class work force whose best feature in the future compared with other nations will be low pay." Kolberg went on to say, "The entire school enterprise needs to be restructured, rethought, and taken more seriously" (*Morning Advocate*, July 1990).

Those in the PC crowd, rather than dealing with the reality of these abysmal test scores and the direction those scores indicate we are headed, prefer to attack the tests and claim that it is impossible to measure a student's real achievement with a standardized test. They also argue that using scores on standardized tests (like the SAT) too rigidly causes teachers to "teach to the test," i.e., teach students how to pass the test. My response to that is, "Hurrah! At least we will be teaching our kids *something*." Another favorite tactic of this group is to attack the tests as being "culturally biased." Those critical of standardized tests in general cite as an example of this bias the word *regatta* being used in the vocabulary section of the SAT. The argument is that only rich, white, country-club kids would know what that word meant. There are, of course, two problems with this argument.

First of all, there is more than one way to know what a regatta is. One way, certainly, is to belong to a club where boat races are held. But another way is to read a book or two. Secondly, and most importantly, the word *regatta* has not appeared on the SAT in over ten years. But, not to be deterred by something like facts, the politically correct crowd is content to brush aside as racist anything that gets in the way of its positions.

I very much resent and categorically reject the PC crowd's accusation that those of us who demand higher academic standards are really racists and that our insis-

tence that such standards are needed is nothing more than
a covert racist agenda, but unfortunately that is the battle
that has been going on in public education across this
country for some time. The statistics cited on the condition
of public education reveal not cultural bias or racism, but
the fact that our system of public education is totally
inadequate in preparing *all* our kids to compete in the high-
tech world and global marketplace of today and tomorrow.
And saying to poor, minority students that all their failures
are simply a result of racism is a pernicious deception.
Raising issues of race to excuse the abominable performance of our system of public education does a grave
disservice not only to that system but, more importantly,
to the students who are the victims of that system. But,
again, the PC crowd on campus uses epithets like *racist,*
sexist, and *homophobe* as carelessly as the McCarthyites
of the fifties used the word *Communist* in order to simply
dismiss those who take issue with their positions.

Those of us who believe in academic standards are
not asking that standards be *raised*; we're simply asking
that some be established. Standards, by definition, are *sup-*
posed to discriminate. If those standards discriminate on
the basis of race, creed, color, or sex, then they are wrong
and they should be changed. But, if they discriminate
against ignorance, apathy, and laziness, then *vive la dis-*
crimination!

Some "professionals" in public education take a somewhat more rational tack and use the pathetic test scores
to argue that cuts in spending on education over the years
are responsible for the poor performance of our public
schools, and that what we really need is *more money!* At
the risk of offending my PC colleagues, such a position
is the result of either ignorance or an intentional effort to
deceive.

Spending on education in this country has increased
steadily over the years from 2.8 percent of our GNP in
1970 to 6.9 percent in 1991. In the 1990-91 academic year,
spending on education was a record 384 billion dollars

($384,000,000,000.00), an increase of almost 7 percent from the previous year. Elementary and secondary schools enjoyed the largest increase, up 7.2% from the previous year to 231 billion dollars ($231,000,000,000.00), and up 34 percent since 1980-81. Per capita expenditures (dollars per student) in grades K through 12 are up 33 percent in the past decade. These increases are *after* adjustments for inflation and are much higher than many of the countries which outperform us in international academic competitions. In fact, in those competitions in which our kids finished 12th in math and 13th in science out of 14 countries, the U.S. fell 2d in terms of funding for education. So, again, the position that we do not spend enough money on education or that funding for education has been cut (some say slashed) simply has no basis in fact. The simple truth is that the problem is not that we do not spend enough money to expect our kids to get an adequate education; the problem is *how* that money is spent. This will be addressed further in chapter 6.

There remains one more point to be considered. Along with grammar, reading, history, and geography, yet another thing we stopped teaching in our schools is values. John R. Silber, president of Boston University, "suggested that higher education was suffering not so much from ideological influence as from a profound relativism" (*Chronicle*, 30 January 1991, p. A-16). The "profound relativism" of which President Silber speaks is at the heart of politically correct thinking, as is the tendency to scoff at traditional values and all things conservative. When asked a question involving a moral choice, the vast majority of my students will answer with two words: "It depends." In the minds of my students, the whole discussion of human morality can be adequately and accurately summarized with these two words, which reflects the "profound relativism" of which President Silber speaks, and that relativism has become more pronounced and widespread through the years that I have been teaching.

Noted scholar Eli Sagan visited our campus recently

and delivered a talk entitled "Cultural Diversity and Moral Relativism." In his talk, Sagan unequivocally makes the link between multiculturalism and the "profound relativism" of which Silber spoke. Sagan said:

> It appears that many, if not the vast majority, of advocates who are impelling us in the direction of cultural diversity, when faced with the question of whether human morality is universal to all people or merely relative to the society in which originates, resoundingly come down on the side of moral relativism. There are no moral universals, we are told; all morality originates in a particular, unique society and is, therefore, relative to that society. There can be no cross-cultural moral discourse, and, most certainly, no culture has the right to sit in judgment on another culture, or even particular aspects of another culture, because such judgment is grounded, not in some universal human condition, but merely in the idiosyncratic cultural position of the particular society making the judgment.

Christina Hoff Sommers, associate professor of philosophy at Clark University in Massachusetts, wrote an article entitled "Ethics Without Virtue." In her piece Professor Sommers criticized the manner in which ethics is approached and taught in American universities today and suggested that the present "crisis" in America, insofar as there is one, "can be attributed to the deterioration of moral education" in the country and to what she called "a hole in the moral ozone." She pointed out that "students taking college ethics are debating abortion, euthanasia, capital punishment, DNA research, and the ethics of transplant surgery while they learn almost nothing about private decency, honesty, personal responsibility, or honor." She further "argued that the current style of ethics teaching which concentrated so much on social policy [which is the demand of the PC/MC crowd] was giving students the wrong ideas about ethics." Professor Sommers maintained that "social morality is only half of the moral life; the other half is private morality, . . ." and she "urged that we attend to both" (*Imprimis*, November 1991, Vol. 20, No. 11, p. 1).

A colleague of Professor Sommers confronted her and told her that she "was wasting her time and even doing harm by promoting bourgeois morality . . . instead of awakening the social conscience of [her] students [a very PC position]." This colleague of Professor Sommers' went on to say that she should "focus on issues of social injustice . . ." like "women's oppression, corruption in big business, multinational corporations and their transgressions in the Third World—that sort of thing." In other words, Professor Sommers was very politically *in*correct.

Professor Sommers saw her colleague at the end of the semester looking "very upset." When she inquired as to what was wrong, her colleague said, "They [her students] cheated on their social justice take-home finals. They plagiarized!" When Professor Sommers asked her what she intended to do, her colleague smiled and said, "I'd like to borrow a copy of that article you wrote on ethics without virtue" (*Imprimis*, p. 1).

Professor Sommers insists that not all students are "dogmatic relativists" or "cheaters and liars," but that "it is impossible to deny that there is a great deal of moral drift." She also reminds us that the course in ethics used to be "a high point of college life," in fact "the culmination of the students' college experience, . . . taken in the senior year and usually taught by the president of the college who would uninhibitedly urge the students to become morally better and stronger" (*Imprimis*, p. 2). But these courses were gradually absorbed by philosophy departments and became just another elective. The 1960s saw a decline in enrollment in ethics courses, but in the late sixties and seventies, such courses enjoyed a renewed popularity.

Sommers, who teaches courses in ethics, said that her "enthusiasm for them [her ethics courses] tapered off when

[she] saw how the students reacted." She revealed that over and over again on evaluation forms, students would say things like, "I learned there was no such thing as right and wrong, just good or bad arguments;" or, "I learned there is no such thing as morality" (*Imprimis*, p. 2). Professor Sommers also admitted that this "moral agnosticism and skepticism" concerned her, and she wanted to understand how her courses might be contributing to this phenomenon. She came to the conclusion that the course content as well as her approach were both contributing factors.

When such issues as "abortion, censorship, capital punishment, world hunger, and affirmative action" were discussed in class, Sommers said that she "naturally felt it [her] job to present careful and well-argued positions on all sides." She decided that "this atmosphere of argument and counterargument was reinforcing the idea that *all* moral questions have at least two sides, i.e., that all of ethics is controversial" and "that ethics itself has no solid foundation" (*Imprimis*, p. 2). The problem, she concluded, is that there is a "relevant distinction . . . between 'basic' ethics and 'dilemma' ethics," a distinction which is no longer made.

Typical instruction in "dilemma ethics" would involve presenting the students with a "problem." A classic dilemma presented to students to consider and discuss would be as follows: The world is about to be destroyed by a meteor; there is a space vehicle which has room for only ten people; who would you take on board and why? Here is an example of a dilemma I have used in my own classes: Lying is wrong; it is Monday morning; a crazed man rushes into the room and points a gun at the student seated in the first desk in the first row; the gunman shouts, "If it's Monday, I'm gonna kill this person! What day is it?" How would you answer the gunman's question?

The typical college course in ethics, Professor Sommers maintains, focuses on presenting problems and dilemmas, such as those just mentioned, which may not have clear-cut answers. This approach could be considered a "deconstructive" analysis of morals and ethics. Professor Sommers contends such approaches create an atmosphere in which "students may easily lose sight of the fact that some things are clearly right and some are clearly wrong, that some ethical truths are not subject to serious debate" (*Imprimis*, p. 2).

Professor Sommers insists "that we [the professoriate] could be doing a far better job of moral education," and that we should be concerned about teaching our students that "a moral life [is] grounded in something more than personal disposition or political fashion." She goes on to quote Samuel Blumenfeld, "You have to be dead to be value neutral," and her response to the question, "Is there really such a thing as *moral* knowledge?" is an "emphatic 'Yes.' To pretend that we know nothing about basic decency, about human rights, about vice and virtue, is fatuous or disingenuous" (*Imprimis*, p. 4).

Echoing Professor Christina Sommers' concern over the "moral drift, agnosticism, and skepticism" so widespread on college campuses and John Silber's consternation over what he calls the "profound relativism" from which higher education is "suffering," Professor Carl Raschke of the University of Denver goes on to say that "he's worried that no one cares about the national increase in violence linked to Satanism." He has written a book entitled *Painted Black: From Drug Killings to Heavy Metal —The Alarming, True Story of How Satanism Is Terrorizing Our Communities,* in which he "describes—in sometimes lurid detail—the 'spreading epidemic of Satanist-related mayhem,' such as drug killings, hate crimes, and adolescent suicide." He also writes, "The American intelligentsia has a tremendous capacity for what psychologists call 'denial.' The trained academic mind has a difficult time accepting that there are people who could willfully do evil for the sake of doing evil,' he adds. 'Evil,

we have been told, is a 'social' or 'structural' disorder to
be remedied by political or therapeutic means" (*Chronicle*,
9 January 1991, p. A-3).

Such approaches have also found their way into our
elementary and secondary schools, because, as Professor
Sommers points out, "so many students come to college
[already] dogmatically committed to a moral relativism
that offers them no grounds" for making decisions regarding their private morality. A popular method of moral
education taught our public school teachers for the past
twenty years is "values clarification," which operates on
the assumption that a teacher should never attempt to
distinguish for the students between right and wrong.

> One favored values clarification technique is to ask
> children about their likes and dislikes: to help them
> become acquainted with their personal preferences.
> The teacher asks the students, 'How do you feel about
> homemade birthday presents? Do you like wall-to-
> wall carpeting? What is your favorite color? Which
> flavor of ice cream do you prefer? How do you feel
> about hit-and-run drivers?' . . . as if one's personal
> preferences in all instances are all that matters. (*Im-
> primis*, p. 3)

Consider one of Professor Sommers' "favorite anecdotes" on this subject.

A sixth grade teacher in Newton, Massachusetts, had
attended several "values clarification" workshops. Remember that this approach to moral education maintains
that teachers should never make distinctions between right
and wrong for their students. It seems that this particular
teacher was "assiduously applying" what she had learned
in the workshops in her class when, one day, her students
announced that they had decided that "they valued cheating and wanted to be free to do it on their tests."

The teacher was not sure how to respond to this
because of her sincere commitment *not* to "indoctrinate"

her students. After thinking about it, the teacher said that because it was *her* class and that *she* was opposed to cheating that they could not cheat *in her class.* "In my class," she said, "you must be honest, for I value honesty. In other areas of your life you may be free to cheat" (*Imprimis*, p. 4).

What the teacher has taught her students, of course, is that it is okay to cheat if you can get away with it, and those "morally bewildered" students will ultimately pay the price for that teacher's decision not to "interfere with" her students' "freedom to work out their own value systems." Professor Sommers concludes her anecdote by declaring that "directive moral education" is "a form of brainwashing," a "pernicious confusion" (*Imprimis*, p. 3).

The results of this approach to "moral education," which "has been popular for the past twenty years," are made clear in an issue of *Time* magazine which revealed the results of surveys that were conducted to discover the most serious discipline problems in our schools. In the 1940s, the most serious problems were talking, chewing gum, running in the halls, getting out of place in line, and not putting paper in the wastebasket. In the 1980s, the problems were drug addiction, alcohol abuse, pregnancy, suicide, rape, robbery, assault, burglary, arson, and bombings. These are our *kids!* These are our *schools! How on earth* could things have come to this?

We are now even experiencing discipline problems at the university. Any number of my colleagues have complained that noise in the hall made by students just "hanging out" constantly disrupts their classes. One of my colleagues in particular, Donald Gill, professor of English, tells of a time when he actually came out of his classroom and asked students sitting around in the hall to be quiet. The students proceeded to taunt Professor Gill, and one even cursed at him, telling him that she "paid [her] tuition and could do what [she] wanted." There were also incidents involving students walking around with "ghetto blasters" blaring in the halls. When I started college, being in one of those buildings was like being in church. Silence was in order, period, end of discussion, but many college kids today have absolutely no sense of decorum.

What is even more appalling than the lack of respect for faculty and the complete disregard for the "rights" of those students who are in class trying to learn is some students' lack of consideration for handicapped students. There are elevators in the building where I work, and there are signs clearly indicating that these were "Reserved for Faculty and Other Handicapped" (I always loved those signs). Yet, not only did young, healthy, ambulatory students disregard these signs, there were so many occasions on which they refused to make room either for students in wheelchairs or for faculty members with audio-visual equipment that the university had to post armed campus police at the entrances of the elevators to enforce the rules. My position is that *the signs shouldn't even be necessary!* Simple courtesy dictates that one who is a healthy biped yield elevator space to people in wheelchairs or faculty members with heavy equipment which prevents them from using the stairs.

This is the end result of "value-free" or "value-neutral" education, which began in the 1960s, became institutionalized in the 1970s, and is now part of what is called "political correctness." The thinking has not changed; even the jargon remains the same; only the name is different. But whether we call it "60s liberalism" or "the decade-old school reform movement" or "political correctness" or "deconstruction" or "multiculturalism," the movement is not at all difficult to trace, and its results are painfully clear; our public schools have become war zones that produce graduates who are simply not prepared to compete in the global market economy of today.

The road back to sanity and competitiveness is not difficult to find nor will it involve spending much more money than we already are. But, you can expect vocal opposition from the PC crowd to every turn we will have to make to get off "the collision course with the reality that America is developing a second-class work force." We need reforms in five specific areas: 1) administration, 2) instruction, 3) curriculum, 4) testing, and 5) values. These reforms will be discussed in detail in chapter 6. For the time being, suffice it to say that our schools must, once again, be about the business of teaching the five R's; that's right, *five*: Reading, 'Riting, 'Rithmatic, Responsibility, and *Respect* (respect for self and for others, especially one's elders).

The last of the five R's, respect, is one, of course, that kids *should* come to school already knowing. Unfortunately, too many of our kids come from abusive and/or broken homes, and the extent to which such conditions have contributed to the problems in our schools is an area that has not received enough attention. Again, risking the ridicule of my PC colleagues, a major contributing factor to these conditions is the welfare system of this country, which, if one is honest, can only be called an economic disaster and a moral disgrace. These programs have victimized the very people they were designed to help, and through these programs, the American taxpayers have subsidized illegitimacy, illiteracy, poverty, profligacy, and the disintegration of the minority family. The effects of these disastrous (albeit well-intentioned) programs have been spilling over into our public schools for some time.

I believed in these programs at first. I believed if we just put enough money into them that we could solve the problems of poverty in this country. But I was wrong. The facts speak for themselves. We have been pouring money into these programs since Lyndon Johnson came up with "The Great Society" back in the 1960s, and in a column I wrote for the *Times of Acadiana* entitled "The Not-So-Great Society," I provided statistical evidence that the situation has actually gotten worse for the people we were trying to help. These programs require substantial reform so that they empower rather than enable, which is what they do now. All our social welfare programs should be based on an understanding of the old adage: If a man is hungry and I give him a fish, he will eat the fish and his hunger will return, but if I teach him to fish, he will never be hungry again. And, as the Rev. Jesse Jackson said, "You're not a man if you can make a baby; you're only a man if you can raise a baby.'"

I participated in a televised panel discussion entitled *Poverty and the Public's Responsibility.* The panel, which was sponsored by the local chapter of the League of Women Voters, consisted of a local newspaper editor, a colleague of mine from the university, a black elected official, and me. When it was my turn to make my presentation, I repeated my recommendations for reforming the welfare program which I had made while campaigning for Congress in 1985-86. I maintain that social welfare programs must be revised so that they provide support for traditional family units rather than demanding the destruction of those units. I believe that we must demand socially responsible behavior from recipients of such benefits, which means doing some kind of work for a welfare check (workfare) or tying benefits to kids' attendance in school (learnfare). I suggest that we limit the number of children of those who receive benefits and the length of time during which one can receive those benefits so that the underclass for whom welfare has become a way of life will stop growing and finally diminish. Needless to say, I was quite alone in my thinking, or at least I felt that way.

In fact, after I had made my remarks, the black elected official attacked me and said, among other things, "Dr. Thibodaux wants to tell me how many children I can have." I said, "No, sir, I don't; but I will tell you how many I'll pay for." There are many demagogues around today who distort the positions of people like me and warn welfare recipients that we would cut off their welfare checks and throw them and their children out into the streets. The fact is that I advocate no such thing. We must maintain our commitment to those victims of the disastrous welfare underclass we have created.

Furthermore, my PC critics love to point out that welfare is a very small percentage of the total budget. My response is that I'm not interested in saving money; I'm interested in improving the quality of life for the underclass our tax dollars have created. The reforms I advocate and have advocated for some time would not save any money in the short term. But if we enact the reforms I suggest *now* and enforce them from this point forward, I believe the problem will begin to correct itself so that twenty years from now this will no longer be an issue. By that time, saving money will simply be an added bonus.

You must understand, of course, that if these proposals make sense to you that you, like me, are very politically *in*correct. You would also be accused, as I have been, of being a racist, which is a convenient transition to a consideration of another of the PC isms: Afrocentrism.

Chapter 3

AFROCENTRISM

Afrocentrism is a very special part of the PC/MC movement. It features a specific ethnic group, Americans of African descent. Afrocentrism seems to have literature and history as its major focus. As mentioned earlier, the politically correct attitude among historians today is to abandon any claims to being definitive or objective for the sake of being "interesting or suggestive" and for the sake of "political agendas." According to *Newsweek* magazine, the agenda of Afrocentrism is "to assert the primacy of traditional African civilizations." Afrocentric scholars assert that "European civilization was derived from Africa" and that "the intellectual history of the West [is] a frantic effort to deny this truth" (*Newsweek*, 23 September 1991, pp. 44-45). Asa Hilliard, professor of psychology and Afro-American history at Georgia State University and a curriculum review consultant for school districts in Portland and New York, asserts that "African history has been lost, stolen, destroyed and suppressed" (*New York Magazine*, 21 January 1991, p. 39). Molefi Kete Assante, chair of the Department of African-American Studies at Temple University and author of the book *Afrocentricity*, maintains, "It's a very simple idea. African people for 500 years have lived on the intellectual terms of Europeans. The African perspective has finally come to dinner" (*Newsweek*, 23 September 1991, p. 42). Professor Assante also asserts that Afrocentrism "is the fastest growing intellectual and practical idea in the community because of its validity" (*Newsweek*, 23 September 1991, p. 46). A few historical personages who were actually black, according to the Afrocentrists, are Jesus, Beethoven, and Robert Browning.

While conventional historical analysis maintains that Western civilization and most of its accomplishments can be traced back to what Edgar Allan Poe called "the glory that was Greece/And the grandeur that was Rome," Afrocentric scholars contend that "accomplishments" regarded as Western in fields ranging from mathematics to architecture to medicine are actually African in origin. Things such as the Pythagorean theorem, the concept of *pi* and other geometric formulas, and the development of the screw and the lever, traditionally thought to have come from Greece, can be traced back even further, to Africa, specifically to Egypt, and the Egyptian civilization, of course, originated in the upper Nile valley on the northeastern border of the African continent.

Perhaps the most significant scholarly work upon which such assertions rest is a book in two volumes (projected as four) entitled *Black Athena* by Martin Bernal. The first volume, published in 1987, won the American Book Award in 1990, and the second volume was published in 1991. Bernal is a professor of government at Cornell University and a scholar of far eastern countries. The thesis of his work is that 18th and 19th century scholars and academics were racists and anti-Semites who intentionally "excised Egypt and Canaan from the family tree of Western civilization" (*Newsweek*, 23 September 1991, p. 49). However, classicist Gregory Crane of Harvard points out that while there is general agreement that the academics Bernal criticizes were, in fact, racist and anti-Semitic, not all scholars accept the notion that personal biases so completely tainted the work of earlier historians. Nevertheless, Bernal maintains that it was the Egyptians and the Phoenicians who "civilized the Aegeans" around 1500 B.C.

Archeological and entomological evidence is the basis of Bernal's assertions. Many Egyptian artifacts, such as coins, jewels, sculpture, and earthenware have been found all across the Aegean area. Sparta used the pyramid as one of its symbols, and a "pyramidlike structure" dating back to 2750 B.C. was found in Thebes. Bernal's grandfather wrote the "definitive Egyptian grammar," and Bernal himself is fluent in Greek, Hebrew, Coptic, Chinese, French, German, Japanese, and Vietnamese. Not only is this impressive, it also certainly lends credibility to his argument that all Greek words are derived from either Egyptian or Semitic.

Scholars dubious of Bernal's conclusions, however, point out that many of the "influences" of which he speaks may well reflect nothing more than trade and cultural ties, and that the "Greeks may well have traced their civilization to Egypt, . . . but only to claim legitimacy through an older civilization, and not because it reflected historical truth." Frank Snowden, a professor emeritus of classics at Howard and "arguably America's greatest black classicist," claims that "when Herodotus, Aeschylus and Aristotle wrote of 'black' Egyptians, they were referring only to their swarthier complexion." Gary Reger, professor of history at Trinity College in Hartford, Connecticut, agrees and says, "Race as an intellectual construct didn't exist" (*Newsweek*, p. 50).

Bernal himself acknowledges that "Egypt has been populated by African, Asian, and Mediterranean [including Semitic] peoples for 7,000 years." He also notes "that ancient carvings usually show Nefertiti with Caucasian features," that "Cleopatra was Greek, not African," and that the upper Nile had "a thoroughly mixed population that got darker and more Negroid the further up the Nile you went" (*Newsweek*, 23 September 1991, p. 50). These admissions, however, point to even more serious scholarly problems for Afrocentrists attempting to assert African ascendancy through Egypt because while Egypt is, indeed, on the African continent, it is actually the southern border of the Mediterranean basin, and its inhabitants are considered "caucasoid," not "negroid." One need only look at Egypt's Hosni Mubarak or Libya's Mummar Al-Qaddafi

to notice the clear physical differences between the inhabitants of the northern coast of Africa and the Negroid
peoples of what used to be called "darkest Africa."

According to the *Encyclopedia Britannica*, "The
Caucasoids of northern and northeastern Africa are related
to the non-African Mediterranean Caucasoids" (Vol. I, p.
281). The map on page 349 of Volume XV of the *Encyclopedia Britannica* demarcating the geographic distribution of "the major races of man" clearly shows that while
Egypt is, indeed, located on the African continent, the
entire north African coast is distinctly "European
(Caucasoid)" and *not* "African (Negroid)."

Furthermore, the swarthy Caucasoid peoples of North
Africa are separated from the darker Negroid peoples to
the south by the expansive and sprawling Sahara Desert.
The map on page 204 of Volume I of the *Encyclopedia
Britannica* showing population distribution clearly indicates just how inhospitable this arid area is. According
to this map, the population is 2.6 persons per square mile
in the *most* populated part of this region.

Britannica points out that race is not merely based
upon superficial physical traits like skin color, facial
features, and hair texture. There are also "less obvious but
more distinctive" genetic differences which show up in
blood types. For instance, according to *Britannica*, "ab-
normal red pigments, such as hemoglobin S (the variant
hemoglobin that is the cause of sickle-cell anemia), which
is rare in most parts of the world . . . [is] found in as many
as half the local residents in some parts of Africa" (p. 352).
The "parts of Africa" where this blood trait is found, of
course, are the southern and central regions where there
are Negroid population. The blood "disorder known as
thalassemia (literally 'sea blood') [which] is apparently
distinctive of people with Mediterranean ancestry" (p.
353) is confined to the Caucasoid peoples of the northern
coast of Africa of the southern Mediterranean Basin. There
are also "genetically determined differences in the excre-
tion of amino acids, . . . genetically determined deficiency

in lactase (an enzyme that helps digest milk sugar), and there are simply inherited differences in earwax type" (p. 352). All this information, of course, makes *Encyclopedia Britannica* very PNC; and I'm sure the PC revisionists will get to work on that posthaste.

I feel it necessary at this point to state categorically that any attempt to interpret any of what I have said as an argument for the superiority of one race over another would be a gross misunderstanding of my point. All I am saying is that all the methods of distinguishing "race," including these new, more scientific ones, offer clear evidence that the differences between the Mediterranean Caucasoids of the North African coast and the Negroid race located further south on the African continent are real and go beyond physical features. But stating factual "differences" does *not* mean that I am implying that one is better or worse than the other.

It is, in fact, the PC Afrocentrists, like Leonard Jefferies, and the PC persons who will call me a racist for daring to point out historical, geographic, and biological facts and genetic differences, who are arguing for the superiority of blacks over whites by "assert[ing] the primacy of traditional African civilizations," specifically Egypt. There are, of course, two glaring problems. The first and most important problem is that the effort to assert the primacy or superiority of one race over another is the very essence of racism. The second problem is that, again, Egypt, while African, is not and has never been considered black or Negroid.

It should also be noted that in addition to the racial and/or genetic distinctions between the people of "Mediterranean" ancestry of North Africa and the Negroid peoples further south, there are significant cultural differences as well. For instance, the "non-African Caucasoids" of the North African coast are, for the most part, followers of Islam or Muslims, and this is not true of the Negroid tribes that live south of the Sahara.

Furthermore, Martin Bernal was quoted as saying that

"the political purpose of *Black Athena* is, of course, to lessen European cultural arrogance" (*Newsweek*, p. 50). While Bernal's credentials certainly give his assertions credibility, such a statement, clearly indicating a "political agenda," would call that credibility into serious question, even though such a "political agenda" is very PC and in line with "new history." As Gertrude Himmelfarb, a historian and professor emeritus at the Graduate School of City University of New York, has already pointed out, "traditional ways of writing history . . . [don't] decide in advance what the pattern of history is going to be for all times and all places" (see chap. 2). In other words, a "political agenda," such as the one "readily acknowledged" by Professor Bernal, would seem to presuppose such "in advance" decisions, which might taint his scholarship. Ironically, this is the same sin of which he accuses earlier academicians.

Another interesting irony of Professor Bernal's work is that he is Jewish, and some of the black Afrocentrists speaking of the "conspiracy" to "steal" African history, technology, art, and culture regard this not only as a white effort, but one that is specifically Jewish. It should be noted that many scholars have detected a strong anti-semitic sentiment in literary deconstructionism. This has been attributed to the fact that Paul De Man, a noted deconstructionist and Derrida's most famous student, was a Nazi. One academic who is constantly quoted speaking of "the long-running conspiracy by Western whites to deny the African contribution to civilization" (*New York Magazine*, 21 January 1991, p. 39) is Professor Leonard Jefferies. This ". . . conspiracy to oppress blacks," according to Professor Jefferies, "stretches from classrooms to the Mafia and Jewish movie producers" (*Newsweek*, 23 September 1991, p. 42). He has also been quoted as saying that ". . . Jews and Italians in Hollywood conspired to denigrate blacks in the movies and that rich Jews played a key role in helping to finance the slave trade" (*Chronicle*, 18 December 1991, p. A-17). Professor Jefferies delivered a

speech in July of 1991 at a black arts festival in Albany,
New York, during which he referred to a colleague of his
at CUNY as "the head Jew." During that same speech,
Jefferies said, "These white folks, even the good ones,
you can't trust" (*Chronicle*, 18 December 1991, p. A-19).

Professor Jefferies has also constructed an anthropo-
logical explanation as to just why whites have oppressed
blacks throughout human history. His theory is that all
human beings are divided into only two categories, "ice
people" (whites) and "sun people" (blacks). The descendants of ice people "are materialistic, selfish, and violent,
while those descended from sun people are nonviolent,
cooperative, and spiritual." Professor Jefferies further
maintains that "blacks are biologically superior to whites
because they have more melanin, and melanin regulates
intellect and health" (*New York Magazine*, 21 January
1991, p. 39).

Some of the comments made by Professor Jefferies
are so boorish I hesitate to include them in this book. I
do, however, believe that it's necessary to include them
in order to demonstrate the caustic tone of the PC movement. Fred Rueckher, a white student who took Jefferies'
class at CUNY, claims that Jefferies "attacked black males
for succumbing to the 'white p— y syndrome,' that is,
pursuing white women." According to Rueckher, Jefferies
also called Diana Ross "an 'international whore' for her
involvement with white men." And he applauded when the
space shuttle Challenger exploded because that "would
deter white people from 'spreading their filth throughout
the universe'" (*New York Magazine*, 21 January 1991, p.
40).

Before Professor Jefferies is dismissed as an extreme
and therefore misleading bit of anecdotal evidence of what
political correctness and multiculturalism has led to, it
should be pointed out that this man is a full professor at
City University of New York where he draws a salary of
over $70,000 a year. He is also the chair of the Department
of Black Studies at CUNY, which now has nine full-time

faculty members. Over one thousand students take classes in this department every semester, and the *Chronicle of Higher Education* reports that students at the University are "either in solidarity with Mr. Jefferies or largely indifferent," and L. Anthony Nieves, a senior at CUNY proclaimed that Jefferies "is sort of like our modern-day Malcolm X" (*Chronicle*, 18 December 1991, p. A-19). He has been called "the future of public education" in the *Boston Herald*, and he has also been "hailed as a hero of the movement to bring Afrocentric ideas into the curriculum" (*Chronicle*, 18 December 1991, p. A-17).

You will also recall that Professor Jefferies was the chief consultant to the New York Board of Regents' Task Force on Minorities, which submitted to the Board the report entitled "One Nation, Many Peoples." The report called for a greater emphasis on multiculturalism in New York public schools, and all the recommendations of this Task Force were adopted by the New York State Board of Education (see chap. 2). According to Bernard Sohmer, professor of mathematics at CUNY, Jefferies' idea of "a multicultural curriculum means leave out everything except black experiences, and then lie about the black experiences" (*Chronicle*, 18 December 1991, p. A-19).

Professor Sohmer is not the only one who has questioned the motives and credibility of Leonard Jefferies. As he became more visible and controversial, his resume' has come under more critical scrutiny. Jefferies calls himself "a consummate scholar," yet his "published scholarship has been practically non-existent since he completed his dissertation [*Sub-National Politics in the Ivory Coast Republic*] and earned his doctorate at Columbia University in 1972." Even Professor Molefi Assante, who "defends Mr. Jefferies, "admits that "it's no secret he [Jefferies] hasn't written any books" (*Chronicle*, 18 December 1991, p. A-19). Sorry, Mr. Assante, but that's what "consummate scholars" do.

For some time, criticism of people like Leonard Jefferies has been nonexistent or merely whispered. I believe that this is because of the fear to criticize blacks or any other member of an ethnic minority—generated by the PC movement. The feeling, however, that *all* scholars, regardless of their race, creed, color, sex, or national origin, should be held to the same standards to which we have always been held and that scholars whose work is shoddy and unprofessional should be exposed and criticized is gaining more and more vocal support. Consequently, Professor Jefferies has recently come under increasing attack, and his position at CUNY, according to recent reports in the *Chronicle,* is tenuous (*Chronicle,* 5 February 1992, A-19). He has been called "anti-white," "anti-Semitic," "a polemicist," "a racial fundamentalist," and "a thug," and his own colleagues at CUNY have called his theories "incoherent" and full of "distortions and half-truths" (*Chronicle,* 18 December 1991, p. A-19). Professor Jefferies' detractors are, however, dismissed by his supporters as "conservatives who oppose a more multicultural curriculum" and as a "white-sheeted mob," once again employing the standard tactic of the PC crowd to simply dismiss any opposition as racist. Furthermore, another result of this kind of thinking and "scholarship" is the tendency to blame each and every failure of any black person on racism. Consider the following examples.

Recently, a black student who was enrolled in one of my classes came to my office for a conference. She had just received a paper back on which she had made a very low grade, and she wanted further clarification as to why. I went over the paper with her in detail, pointing out errors I had already marked and then reiterated the comments that I had written at the end of her paper. The student said that she really hadn't understood the assignment and that she had followed a classmate's directions. I told her that she should have come to me if she had any questions. She said, "Well, I knew that you are a Republican, so you don't like black people."

Now, I know that when it comes to politics, perception is reality. I am also well aware that this student's perception

is the one that liberals, Democrats, and the media have
worked very hard to create. One need only analyze the
returns of any election to know that the efforts to establish
this perception as fact have been very successful, but as
far as our students are concerned, one of the things we
are *supposed* to teach at the freshman level is that stereotypical thinking is unfair, simple-minded, not analytical,
and to be avoided. But these circumstances reveal the
fundamental hypocrisy of the PC movement because,
apparently, it's okay to apply stereotypical thinking to
PNC persons, like Republicans.

Nevertheless, I gave my student the spiel about the
history of the GOP as the party of Lincoln, abolition, and
free blacks, and of my own work with the Louisiana
Council on Human Relations. I also pointed out that on
the very first official celebration of Martin Luther King,
Jr.'s birthday, I was the *only* faculty member, black or
white, to participate in the march across our campus. The
student was, of course, not convinced. In fact, she took
the occasion to inform me that I had offended her by
assigning a short story by Theodore Dreiser entitled "Nigger
Jeff." I must admit I was stunned because the story is a
very traditional, anti-racist piece about a black man being
lynched by an angry, white mob. "Oh," she said, "I didn't
know that." It turns out that she hadn't even read the story.

Well, the student did not drop my class, which I
expected her to do. She, instead, stayed in, worked hard,
and passed. She came to me at the end of the semester
and said that she had come close to dropping my class
but was glad that she had not because she had been forced
to re-think some of the things she had been told and had
merely accepted. I guess we must be grateful for small
victories, and that is, indeed, a very small victory in the
face of all that is going on.

Recently two of my colleagues have been accused of
being racists by black students who claim that their grades
were a result of racism (see chap. 7). Many of my colleagues have similar stories to tell, but the most famous

(or infamous) example of this tendency to blame every failure of any black individual on racism occurred early in 1989 when Coach John Thompson of Georgetown walked off the basketball court in the middle of a nationally televised game. This was Thompson's way of protesting the NCAA's Proposition 42, which, the coach insisted, was racist.

Proposition 42 would have made an athlete ineligible for a scholarship if his/her grade point average were below 2.0 on a four-point scale, which is the lowest average a student can have and still have a C. The student/athlete would also have been ineligible for scholarship under Prop 42 if he/she failed to achieve a minimum composite score of 700 on the SAT (Scholastic Aptitude Test) or 15 on the ACT (American College Test). Athletes who did not meet these minimum requirements were already ineligible to play as freshman even before Proposition 42.

You might be wondering how difficult it would be to achieve these minimum requirements. So let us consider what one would have to do to score a 700 on the SAT. It should first be noted that even if a student missed *every single question*, that student would still score a 200. Nevertheless, at the time that Thompson made his protest, there were sixty questions on the math section of the SAT and eighty-five questions on the verbal section. To achieve the minimum requirements specified under the NCAA's Proposition 42, one would have to answer thirteen questions correctly on the math section and twenty-four questions correctly on the verbal section. What this means is that a student would have to score a 13/60 in math and a 24/85 in verbal. That's a 21.6 percent in math and a 28.2 percent in verbal. This is what Coach Thompson considered racist. Did I miss something?

Three specific charges were made. First, the SAT and ACT tests are culturally biased (sound familiar?). Second, these kinds of standards are really designed to keep poor black kids out of the university. Third, the ultimate goal of Proposition 42 was to prevent blacks from dominating both collegiate and professional sports. Again, this kind of thinking is typical of the PC crowd on campus. As I have already stated, the fact that American kids cannot even reach such pitifully minimal standards on college exams is, to me, an indication not of cultural bias but of the incredible failure of public education in this country. But, people like me who take issue with a PC position are simply called "racist" and, *presto*, their position is rendered irrelevant, facts notwithstanding.

Before the impact that this politically correct movement toward multiculturalism, generally, and Afrocentrism, specifically, is underestimated, consider the following excerpts from a guest column written for and published in the student newspaper at the university where I work.

> . . . It is time African-American men stand up to this white racist society . . .
> . . . America is a country built on racism, discrimination and quotas. Four hundred years of free slave labor was the key factor which made this country the so-called great nation it is today. . . .
> Affirmative Action and quotas are insults to African-Americans viewing the opportunities and freedoms their ancestors have been denied, and are still being denied, since the time your racist forefathers created this vicious system to keep African-Americans oppressed.

This editorial was published in the student paper on 25 October 1991. Surely the echoes of Professor Jefferies and Afrocentrism are clear. The author of this column went on to coauthor another such diatribe with a young man which was published in the student paper 8 November 1991. Consider the following excerpts from that piece.

> In the dawn of early America, our African ancestors were placed in bondage by Europeans and brought to these shores to be slaves. The Africans were to endure 250 years of systematic breeding, brainwashing and genocide. . . .

Today, African-Americans are still faced with
slavery—MENTAL SLAVERY. . . .The American
system, which was created out of the racist ideology
of Europeans, further developed the mental slavery
among African-Americans and continues to do so
today. . . .
    One of the key elements Europeans used to
contribute to the slave mentalities of African-Americans was religion. Presently, European religion,
'Christianity,' remains the key element keeping
African-American minds in bondage. . . .
    History documents that the teachings of the Bible
and Christianity are actually derived from the writings of ancient African priests, rulers, and philoso-
phers. Ancient African texts document the first stories
of the Annunciation, the Immaculate Conception, the
Virgin Birth and the world's first Savior, who was
proclaimed as the Son of God. All of the documents
were written over 4,000 years before the birth of the
Christian Son of God, "Jesus the Christ. . . ."
    African-Americans, and many others who call
themselves "Christians," must realize that their
religion is nothing more than a European version of
African philosophy and religious thought.

These are college students, and this is what they have
learned in college, and the college is not a big east- or
west-coast institution but an average size school in the
south. Some of the comments contained in these two
columns are, indeed, accurate, but if there are assertions
made and conclusions drawn that strike you as, to say the
least, odd, don't be concerned. Any normal human being
would find much that is in these two columns strange if
not outrageous, and those assertions that appear to be so
have either no scholarly basis at all or rest on evidence
which is, at best, inconclusive. Dr. Gary Marotta points
out that the second piece is not only historically inaccurate,
it is a contradiction in terms (see chap. 7). Yet the assertions
are made as statements of fact, and this is typical of
politically correct thinking because when "political agendas" become more important than history itself, one does

not need to let facts or the lack of scholarly evidence get
in the way of one's assertions. If history does not serve
the purposes of displaced, oppressed minorities, it is simply
changed.

Consider an editorial which also appeared in the student newspaper on 31 January 1992. The title of the
column was "Schools Choose to Eliminate Important
Historical Records." The author of the column admits that
she "did not even know that Egypt was a part of Africa"
and uses this as proof of the Afrocentric theory that "the
intellectual history of the West [is] a frantic effort to deny
[the] truth" that "European civilization was derived from
Africa." For starters, I would challenge the writer to carefully
analyze the statistics on the geographical knowledge of
all Americans in her age group contained in Chapter 2
of this book which clearly reveal the fact that *very few*
of our kids know where *anything* is. I would then go even
further and challenge the accuracy of some of her statements. For instance, she writes that "the historian Herodotus
. . . described distinctly the Ancient Egyptians as persons
with Negroid characteristics." She also states that "Cheops
and Nefertiti have Negroid features" and that "Negroid
peoples have always been denied their history and recognition of their contributions to society because of the
trans-Atlantic slave trade." She concludes by saying that,
"I have come to the belief that history in the school system
sometimes chooses to eliminate important records and
documents of past events. I have come to believe that since
the trans-Atlantic slave trade, history has been used di-
dactically to keep an oppressed people neglected of their
history, thus making it hard for them to deal with their
own present."

The statements of this writer, as with the two previous
columnists, are, at best, disputable, at worst, wrong. The
ultimate question for academics, of course, is that once
students "come to believe" the notions this student has
accepted, are they still open to facts which would refute
their "beliefs," or would they be more inclined to regard

such "facts" as just more racist propaganda? If the latter is the case, how does one teach such students?

As with multiculturalism generally, Afrocentrism has also trickled down into the elementary and secondary levels of public education. Again I refer to ABC's "Nightline" program which was devoted to discussing the impact that all this has had on instruction of history in public schools. One of the guests on that program, who has already been mentioned, was Professor Manning Marable of the University of Colorado. Professor Marable said on that program

> The way we should teach the American Revolution or the Civil War is by focusing on themes that cut across various ethnic communities, that find unity within diversity. So, if we're talking about the issue of freedom, we can talk about Patrick Henry's "Give Me Liberty or Give Me Death" speech before the American Revolution, but we can also talk about the freedom that is spoken of by Martin Luther King in the *Letter from the Birmingham Jail.* We can talk about democracy that's expressed in the Declaration of Independence, but we can also see democratic ideals in the writings of a Frederick Douglas, the great black abolitionist.

The only problem is that Martin Luther King and Frederick Douglas were not around during the American Revolution, and to mention either one of them while teaching that period in American history would be to violate the historical context.

Nevertheless, Professor Marable went on to point out that, "History and culture are learned; they're not genetic. So, simply because a student is Mexican-American, that doesn't mean that she will know about *Cinco de Mayo* or that simply because a student is black, he'll know the words to 'Lift Ev'ry Voice and Sing.'" That seemed to me to be a logical point, but the extension of that point is that simply because a student is white, that doesn't mean that he or she will know about James Madison. I decided to test this out.

The day after the "Nightline" broadcast, I asked my sons a few questions. My oldest son is a junior in high school, and my youngest son is in the sixth grade. My youngest son happened to have a friend over who is also in the sixth grade, and they all attend public schools. All three of them knew the name of Crispus Attucks and that he died in the American Revolution. My oldest son went further and said, "He was the first man to die in the struggle for independence." Now, historically speaking, my son's statement, which makes this man sound like a soldier in the Revolutionary army, is not accurate. To be completely accurate, Crispus Attucks, who was black, died as a result of random shooting when a group of British soldiers opened fire on a crowd of colonists. The colonists, who were intentionally trying to force a confrontation, had been taunting and throwing rocks at the soldiers and had refused to disperse after being ordered several times to do so. Only four people died in the episode, which became known as The Boston Massacre. As the name of the incident suggests, it was blown out of proportion and became a major propaganda tool for the patriots who were calling for separation from England. Now you would think that calling one of the most famous episodes in the American Revolution a "propoganda tool" for our side would be very PC. But these people are *never* satisfied. Nevertheless, all the kids knew who Crispus Attucks was.

Then my daughter, who is in eighth grade, returned home from a friend's house and came into the room. The boys didn't want her included because they said she would know all the answers, but they acquiesced under my disapproving look. She also knew who Crispus Attucks was. Only my oldest son knew who Patrick Henry was. When I asked them who the "Father of the Constitution" was, they all said Thomas Jefferson. In fact, Thomas Jefferson was out of the country during the Constitutional Convention, serving as an emissary to France. The "Father of the

Constitution" was James Madison. The two sixth graders did not know who James Madison was. Although my older son and my daughter did know the name of James Madison, they were not sure who he was. Now, I ask any intelligent, honest person to answer the following question: Who is more important in the ultimate scheme of the history of the American Revolutionary period—Crispus Attucks or James Madison? That is *not* to say that I mind that my kids know who Crispus Attucks was. I'm glad that they do, although I am somewhat concerned about my older son's rather distorted view of his role in the "struggle for independence." I am, however, outraged that they did not know who James Madison was. By the way, they do now.

On to the Civil War. All the kids knew Harriett Tubman and Frederick Douglas. None of them had heard of Generals McClellan or Meade or the battles of Vicksburg or Shiloh, and the sixth graders had not heard of Grant or Bull Run. My daughter said that they would learn that in seventh grade. Okay, fine, but the point is that Professor Marable's position, which is the PC multiculturalist position, that minority contributions are being excluded from the classroom clearly has no basis in fact. That may have been true of the 1950 classroom, but it is certainly not true of the 1990 classroom. Not only are minority perspectives being included, they are being taught *first*, at the risk of distorting the larger picture. And I don't need anyone to tell me that my method is not scientific. I know that my kids do not constitute a scientific sample, but they are average kids in average schools, and they are part of those horrendous statistics on public education mentioned in chapter 2.

I would also mention as an interesting aside that I was watching the television game show "Wheel of Fortune" just a couple of days after I had seen the "Nightline" program. For those who are unfamiliar with this program, three contestants attempt to solve puzzles by calling out letters. Each contestant takes turns spinning the wheel which lands on a dollar amount. The contestant then calls out a letter, and if the letter called out by the contestant is in the puzzle, the letter is turned and that contestant's turn continues. If the letter called out is not in the puzzle, then the wheel is spun by the next contestant, who calls a letter, and so on. Any contestant can solve the puzzle at any time in their turn. The puzzles are identified by a "category." Sometimes, the category is "clue," which means that the solution to the puzzle is a clue to another answer. If the contestant who solved the puzzle can give the answer of the clue as well, he or she wins an additional $500. If that contestant cannot answer or answers incorrectly, the next contestant gets a chance to win the $500, and if that contestant is wrong, then the last contestant gets a chance to win the money. Coincidentally, the "clue" puzzle this particular evening was "Give Me Liberty or Give Me Death." All any of the contestants had to do to win $500 was to give the name of the person who said this, and, you guessed it, nobody knew the answer! And these were all adults!

I would also add, by the way, that all my kids knew a great deal about Martin Luther King, and I would venture to say that if "Wheel of Fortune" ever has "I Have a Dream" as its "clue" puzzle, somebody will win that $500. That is not to say that I mind that people everywhere and of all ages know who Martin Luther King, Jr., was. But, the PC crowd doesn't seem to mind that so few people know who Patrick Henry was. In fact, I am convinced that some of them would actually be glad that Patrick Henry seems to be fading into historical oblivion. That's one less dead white male they'll have to worry about.

Not only have the curricula been changed to accommodate PC multicultural/Afrocentric demands, there are entire schools and school districts being taken over. According to *Newsweek*, "No one knows exactly how many schools describe themselves as 'Afrocentric,' although educators agree that the number is growing" (23 September 1991, p. 45). According to the *Chronicle of Higher Edu-*

cation, "New York, Minneapolis, and Detroit have announced that they will follow Milwaukee's lead and set up Afrocentric schools devoted to the special needs of minority-group students" (6 February 1991, p. A-6). In Detroit and Milwaukee, "the demands for Afrocentric curriculum . . . have gone beyond the trend toward multiculturalism and sought instead to create blacks-only male academies." Imagine the furor if white parents made similar demands. How about a "United White College Fund" or a "Miss White America Pageant"? Still, in Atlanta, Georgia, black parents have the option of sending their kids to the Afrocentric Atlanta Preparatory School. Gail Goodman, who enrolled her twelve-year-old daughter in the new school, said, "I don't have any problem with integration, but our children have to be prepared, and we want her to know both sides. It's like going into a war" (*Newsweek,* 23 September 1991, p. 42).

And what do these Afrocentric schools teach? At the Shule Mandela Academy in East Palo Alto, California, for instance, the school's students, who are all black, "pledge to 'think black, act black, speak black, buy black, pray black, love black, and live black.'" This is done every morning during *mkutano* (the Kiswahili word for assembly). If whites did this, wouldn't that be called racism? Nevertheless, also during *mkutano,* "Students sing Bob Marley, not Francis Scott Key. They recite Langston Hughes, not Vachel Lindsay" (*Newsweek,* 23 September 1991, p. 45). Dr. Charles Finch of the Morehouse School of Medicine proclaims, "Blacks must reconstruct their historical memory. No nation, no race can face the future unless it knows what it is capable of. This is the function of history" (*Newsweek,* p. 42). This, however, as pointed out in the *Newsweek* article, is the proper function of myth, not history. Nevertheless, James Turner, founder of Africana Studies at Cornell, asks, "What is school if it doesn't build children's self-confidence? American education does that for white children. From the day white kids walk into

school, they are told that they are heirs to the greatest
achievements of humankind" (*Newsweek*, p. 44).

There are two problems with such statements. First of
all, as the *Newsweek* article asks, tongue-in-cheek, "Does
anyone really believe that white children draw inspiration
from their kinship to Isaac Newton?" (p. 44). According
to our kids' test results, I think it would be safe to say that
if you were to ask them who Isaac Newton was, the vast
majority of them wouldn't even be able to answer you,
and, of the ones who would answer, some would probably
say he was a Las Vegas nightclub singer. On a more serious
note, Professor Diane Ravitch of Columbia maintains that
"the idea that children can learn only from the experiences
of people from the same race represents a sort of racial
fundamentalism" (*New York Magazine,* 21 January 1991,
p. 40). But the PC crowd doesn't even stop there. They
not only want kids taught "the experiences of people from
the same race," they want it taught only by teachers from
the same race as well.

When I presented my paper criticizing political correctness and its "isms" at the Louisiana Association for
College Composition at Northeastern Louisiana University
in October of 1991, I was asked during the discussion after
the presentation of papers if I would "object to black
students demanding that black history be taught by black
teachers." I responded by asking if that meant that white
students had the right to demand that "white" history be
taught by white teachers. Dr. Gary Marotta, Vice President
of Academic Affairs at the university where I work, also
addressed this issue in an article he wrote back in 1977
entitled "Cultural Pluralism: Promises and Problems." In
that article, Professor Marotta quotes Bayard Rustin, President of the A. Philip Randolph Institute, who said, "To
suggest that because a black child is taught by a black
teacher he or she will receive better education than if taught
by a white . . . is sheer nonsense: it has no basis in fact
and furthermore entails some dangerous implications"

("Ethnics: A New Separatism," *New York Teacher Magazine,* March, 1972, p. 2). Dr. Marotta also wrote in that early piece that "misconceptions spawned by pluralism were distorting educational policy."

In his interview with me, I asked Dr. Marotta if he thought that PC multiculturalism was distorting educational policy today. His response was, "Yes. I think there's no question. I think that what I pointed to as a potential problem [in 1977] has actualized itself. It leads to things like Afrocentric studies. These areas merit study, but they should be infused into existing curricula and should not be ghettoized. We are reinventing ethnic and racial apartheid, and it's a mistake" (see chap. 7).

Professor Ravitch also points out that "the success of Chinese students in math is due not to a 'Sinocentric' approach to numbers but to hard work." She goes on to say that "if the 'self-esteem' model had any validity, Italian American students—the descendants of Caesar and Michelangelo—would excel in school, but in fact they have the highest drop-out rate of any white group in New York City schools" (*New York Magazine,* 21 January 1991, p. 40). Furthermore, Professor Ravitch also contends that "asking history curricula to raise the self-esteem of minority children opens up a Pandora's box of demands to include nothing that is critical of particular groups" (*Chronicle,* 6 February 1991, p. A-6).

As a case in point, thanks to Alex Haley and Hollywood, the perception has been created that all slaves were simply pure children of nature who, while wandering about in the forest one day, suddenly found themselves hanging from a tree in a net and, after a long boat ride, then found themselves singing "Swing Low, Sweet Chariot" on a plantation in Georgia. Nowhere is it mentioned that many Africans themselves dealt with the white slave traders and that blacks often sold each other into slavery. Should that be taught in Afrocentric schools? It should if one is interested in history as a chronology of significant events and as the "disinterested pursuit of the truth" rather than just as a political tool. The fact is that just as the Holocaust is a *human* tragedy and not just a Jewish one, so too is slavery a disgrace in human history and not just a "black" experience. But teaching that anything bad could have come out of Africa is very, very politically incorrect.

Pulitzer Prize winning historian Arthur Schlesinger, Jr., maintains that what Afrocentric scholars are "saying, essentially, is that Africa is the source of all good and Europe is the source of all evil" (*Newsweek*, 23 September 1991, p. 42). Lynne Cheney, chair of the National Endowment for the Humanities, agrees and says, "There seems to be a central theme that anything that happens in the West is bad and everything out of Africa is good" (*Newsweek*, p. 46). Frank Snowden of Howard and "arguably America's greatest black classicist," said, "Many students have already been misled and confused by Afrocentrists' inaccuracies and omissions in their treatment of blacks in the ancient Mediterranean world. The time has come for Afrocentrists to cease mythologizing and falsifying the past. The time has come for scholars and educators to insist upon scholarly rigor and truth in current and projected revisions of our curriculum. *Tempus fugit!*" (Measure, No. 102, Jan. 1992, p. 10).

Former Secretary of Education William Bennett says he is offended by the "anti-white tone" of the whole Afrocentric movement and also calls it "anti-American." Bennett goes on to say, "I think it will further alienate the poor who are already tenuously connected to American culture" (*Newsweek*, p. 46). Arthur Schlesinger warns, "Afrocentrism in the schools is a symptom of a growing fragmentation that is threatening to divide our society" (*Chronicle*, 6 February 1991, p. A-6).

In spite of the august names already cited in the list of critics and opponents of Afrocentrism and the politically correct multicultural drift in public education in this country today, some of the most impressive have not yet been mentioned. One is that of Henry Louis Gates, Jr., a black man, who began his academic career at Cornell University, was "wooed away" by Duke University to become a professor of literature, and was then sought out by Harvard University where he is presently a professor of English and the chairman of Afro-American Studies. Not only is Professor Gates one of the most renowned scholars in black studies in America today, "known for his work establishing and analyzing the Afro-American literary canon," he was, originally, one of the strongest proponents for multicultural research in the humanities and was himself one of the pioneers of such research. However, Gates and two other "pioneers" in multicultural research, Cornel West, professor of philosophy and Afro-American studies at Princeton University, and Gayatri Chakravorty Spivak of the University of Pittsburgh, have now "faulted recent multicultural scholarship for: a 'politics of style' that has substituted oversimplified rhetoric and literary theory for an analysis of society; a 'particularism' that has divided researchers into separate camps; and a 'political correctness' that has avoided self-criticism" (*Chronicle*, 28 November 1990, p. A-5).

Professor West said, "We need to provide some analytic content" (*Chronicle*, p. 5). Professor Spivak seemed to agree with Bennett when he "suggested that the emphasis many scholars place on the marginality of women and members of minority groups has served to reinforce their place on the margins of culture" (*Chronicle*, p. A-8). Professor Gates also echoed William Bennett's assessment when he said, "It is time to ask how well it [multicultural research] has addressed the problems of the groups it had sought to help" (*Chronicle*, p. A-5). Gates went on to maintain that, "Today, routinized righteous indignation has been substituted for rigorous criticism," and that multicultural scholarship has "created a windily apocalyptic rhetoric that had nowhere to go when its punitive demands were granted" (*Chronicle*, p. A-8).

Of African-American studies, specifically, Gates warned that "those in our field must remember that we are scholars first, not polemicists." He called for "a true

proliferation of rigorous methodologies rather than . . .
ideological conformity." Gates also said that "we should
not lay claim to the idea of 'blackness' as an ideology or
religion" and that "African-American studies is not just
for blacks." He then asked, "What would we say to a
person who said that to teach Milton, you had to be Anglo-
Saxon, Protestant, male, and blind!" Gates also chuckled
at the irony of Afrocentric scholars who, after so vilifying
Western culture, then go to such great lengths "to
claim authorship" of all its achievements. He went on
to call Leonard Jefferies' "theories of 'sun' and 'ice'
people . . . bogus," and added that "the invidious
scapegoating of other ethnic groups only resurrects the
worst 19th-century racist pseudoscience—which too many
of the pharaohs of 'Afrocentrism' have accepted without
realizing" (*Newsweek*, 23 September 1991, p. 47).

I concur absolutely with Professor Gates, and I say
"Thank God!" that a prominent *black* scholar had the
courage to speak the truth about politically correct
multiculturalism and Afrocentrism, which is to say that
much of it is as racist as anything humanity has ever
concocted. It is as unfortunate as it was necessary that this
point be made by a *black* scholar.

I think that Arthur Schlesinger's comment that
"Afrocentrism in the schools is a symptom of a growing
fragmentation that is threatening to divide our society" also
drives to the very heart of the matter. The politically correct
movement (and all its attendant "isms") is, above all else,
confrontational and divisive. It is rendered so by its very
premise, for one cannot have a history of oppression
without having oppressor/villains and oppressed/victims.
The oppressor/villains are, of course, simply by the process
of elimination, white males of European descent and
virtually everything associated with the Western culture
they produced. This whole notion is, by the way, nothing
but a warmed over version of Marxism, which also rested
on such an "interpretation" of history, i.e., oppressed/
working masses being manipulated by oppressor/owners

of the means of production. One need only witness what is happening in Eastern Europe and what used to be the Soviet Union to see how valid such "interpretations" of history are. And, as Professor Diane Ravitch points out, "By promoting a brand of history in which everyone is either a descendant of victims or oppressors, ancient hatreds are fanned and re-created in each new generation" (*New York Magazine*, 21 January 1991, p. 40). In this, political correctness, *et al.*, does a grave disservice to our country and our culture, because in the land of *e pluribus unum*, we could use a lot less *pluribus* and a lot more *unum*.

Another interesting aspect about this PC mentality as regards race is the tendency that PC persons have to dismiss any black, like Professor Gates, who dares to speak against their agenda as "Uncle Toms." What is even more interesting is that blacks do this to each other. I know this because black friends and students have told me that it is so. I recently attended a banquet, and the guest speaker was Ben Carson, who is black and the director of pediatric neurosurgery at Johns Hopkins University. Dr. Carson remarked that his white patients accept him more readily than do some of his black patients. He said that the general reaction of white patients to him is, "Wow, this guy must be something really special." His black patients, on the other hand, generally react with, "I don't want no affirmative action operatin' on my brain." Dr. Carson called this the "crabs in the barrel" syndrome. He said that if you put a bunch of crabs in a barrel and one starts to crawl out, the others reach up and pull him back down. This was his analogy for the "Uncle Tom" mentality among blacks. I have tremendous respect for articulate, successful, middle-aged blacks because these are people who have not only found the courage and strength to rise above the *real* discrimination of the fifties and sixties, but who have also had to deal with being ostracized by the people of their own race as "Uncle Toms." In other words, as Professor Gates suggested, white Europeans are not the only ones capable of being racists.

To be sure, racism existed in this country, and it still does. Unfortunately, it always will. It cannot be legislated or taught out of existence. All that can be done is to prevent it from becoming institutionalized as a matter of law as it once was. All you can reasonably do to accomplish that is to make any kind of discrimination illegal, which we have done, and provide legal recourse for those who can prove that they are victims of such discrimination, which we have done. And we have done this to the extent that, as Professor Dennis of Columbia points out, "the letter of the law on matters like affirmative action, anti-harassment, and other socially desirable initiatives long ago outdistanced the spirit of the law and the rationale behind rules that were offered up to improve the quality of life" (*War of Words*, p. 12). In other words, what we are doing today is attempting to redress historical grievances which involves penalizing people today for the sins of their ancestors, and that is as inherently unfair as were the initial wrongs.

I tried this theory out in one of my freshman literature classes. Being the racist, conservative, right-wing, Eurocentric homophobe that I am, I always teach *The Odyssey* to my freshman. I always give the background as well, which includes the story of Thyestes and Atreus. I cannot go into all the details here, so the following quick summary will have to suffice. Atreus was named king of Mycenae, and the jealous Thyestes gets back at his brother by encouraging the queen to be unfaithful. Atreus retaliates for this treachery by banishing his brother from the kingdom.   Later, Atreus pretends to forgive his brother and has him over to dinner. Unbeknownst to Thyestes, his brother has kidnapped and killed his children, and Atreus feeds the slain children to their father as the main course. Thyestes, understandably upset, then places a curse on his brother's house, i.e., on all his descendants. Atreus' sons were Agamemnon and Menelaus. Now Menelaus took as his wife the beautiful Helen. She, of course, was kidnapped from her husband's house by Paris who took Helen to his home, Troy. After the decade-long Trojan War, which was accompanied by much suffering and death, Menelaus finally got his wife back and returned to his home in Sparta. When Agamemnon returned home, he was murdered by his unfaithful wife and her lover, Aegisthus. And this cycle of violence and vengeance goes on and on, and people continue to suffer for the sins of their ancestors. The class agreed that this was unjust and that at some point in time, somebody would have to "give it up" and "let it go" so everybody could just get on with their lives, and the black students in the class were the most vocal in expressing this opinion.

I am very sorry that the institution of slavery ever existed in this country. It should not have. But I never owned a slave, nor did my parents, nor did my grandparents, nor did my great grandparents. Nor is there a black person born in America alive today who was ever a slave, and because the institution of slavery ceased to exist in this country almost one hundred and thirty years ago, I think you would be hard pressed to find many people in this country whose knowledge of slavery is anything more than historical. I am equally sorry that there was ever legalized, institutionalized racial discrimination in this country. That too was wrong, and it should never have existed. Having said that, we must understand that sooner or later, we're simply going to have to move on and leave all the old hatreds and resentments behind. That will not happen until we drop all the ethnic labels and categorizing and stop the racial scapegoating and perceive of ourselves first as human beings, second as Americans, and whatever else after that.

Chapter 4

GENDERISM

Another of the "isms" spawned by the politically correct movement is a radical form of feminism which has come to be known as "gender feminism" or "genderism." If you have found PC multiculturalism and Afrocentrism shocking, you're gonna love this one. The "rallying cry" of the gender feminists is, "To know is to f —k!" (*New York Magazine*, 21 January 1991, p. 38). The basic premise of genderism is "that Western society is organized around a 'sex/gender system'." In my opinion, just as multiculturalism and Afrocentrism crash head-first into the wall of historical fact, the politically correct genderists run head-first into scientific fact.

According to Sandra Harding, a professor of philosophy at the University of Delaware and a proponent of this particular politically correct "ism," central to this sex/gender system "is male dominance made possible by men's control of women's productive and reproductive labor" (*New York Magazine*, 21 January 1991, p. 38). So, as you might expect, abortion is one of the first issues raised by this segment of the PC crowd. Of course, the euphemistic "pro-choice" position is the politically correct one. Here, again, the PC movement runs afoul of one of the principles composition teachers are supposed to teach their students, which is: don't use euphemisms. Well, I will practice what I preach and call the "pro-choice" position what it actually is, i.e., pro-abortion.

Because the abortion issue is so emotional (on both sides), there seems to be little room for calm, rational discussion based on scientific fact. The whole issue of abortion revolves around one simple question: What is a fetus? If it is an "unviable tissue mass," which is what the pro-abortion forces have always maintained, then removing it is no different from removing a tumor. If that is the case, no big deal. But if a fetus is a human life, then the discussion takes on a whole new dimension.

I might also point out that not all those who are pro-abortion are PC liberals. There is a growing number of people who call themselves "Republicans for Choice" who claim to oppose making abortion illegal, and the reason they give is that a true conservative opposes all government interference in people's lives. This is taking conservatism to an extreme because no conservative that I know of argues that government has *no* legitimate role to play in our lives. That is anarchism, not conservatism. Any intelligent conservative knows and admits that government does, indeed, have a legitimate role to play in our lives, not the least of which involves protecting all of our rights against those who would deprive us of them, and that is why in this country, no one has the moral or legal right to "choose" to deprive another human being of "life, liberty or property without due process of law." But the PC crowd has reduced the Constitution to "the embodiment of the White Male with Property Model," so I suppose its concepts are irrelevant anyway. And then there's the deconstructive game of trying to determine what "life" is, and, even more fun, when it begins.

For some time, an arbitrary line in the sand was drawn at the end of the first trimester as the demarcation marking the beginning of "life." Of course, advances in medical technology continued to force those who stood on that line to retreat further and further toward the beginning of gestation. For instance, it has been established that a fetus has brain waves which can be measured by EEG only 40 days after conception, and merely 18 days after conception, the fetus has a measurable heart beat. In fact, they were getting so close to the beginning of gestation, i.e., conception, that the PC pro-abortion genderists then had to adopt the more ephemeral "viability" position. Of course, according to their definition of "viability," comatose patients would not be considered human beings because, in some ways, a fetus is actually more "viable" than someone who is comatose. As obstetrical and gynecological medicine continued its inevitable advance, revealing more and more about the nature of a human fetus, the pro-abortion forces continued their retreat until now they do not even discuss the fetus at all. As with all politically correct positions, if a fact gets in the way, it is simply changed or ignored.

Unfortunately for the pro-abortion genderists, the fetus is a fact, a fact which is itself usually the result of "choices." Furthermore, the simple scientific fact is that at the moment of conception, the embryo is *not* a part of the mother's body. At that point and forever more it is a genetically distinct being with its own genetic code that is completely and totally different from every other human being who has ever lived or ever will live, including the mother. So here is the first instance of PC genderism crashing into scientific fact.

It also seems ironic that while more and more law enforcement agencies in this country are now turning to DNA identification in criminal investigations and our courts are now admitting such identification as evidence in criminal prosecution, the rights of a fetus, which has its own, distinct DNA code at the moment of conception, are still not legally recognized in all cases. Now they are recognized in *some* cases, for there have been instances of people being prosecuted for two murders when they have killed pregnant women. There are also cases where mothers who have given birth to babies who are addicted to illegal drugs have been prosecuted, but there are no consistent standards or guidelines. It is also a macabre irony that in this country it is illegal to destroy the egg of an American bald eagle, but the government uses our tax dollars to destroy human embryos and fetuses.

But again, never to be deterred by scientific evidence, medical fact, or legal precedent, the politically correct genderists simply ignore the reality and existence of the fetus and maintain that it is impossible to ascertain when human life actually begins. The problem with this position, assuming one is interested in constructing a rational argument, is that it contains the admission that abortion just *might* be the killing of a human being. That raises two logical questions: (1) What are the consequences if the pro-abortion forces are wrong? and (2) What are the consequences if the pro-life forces are wrong? If the pro-abortion forces are wrong, and the fetus *is* a human life, then, simply in terms of sheer numbers, this enterprise in which we have been involved since the *Roe v. Wade* decision is a holocaust which makes the Nazi murders pale by comparison.

If it turns out that the pro-life advocates are wrong, and the fetus is *not* a human being, then the lives of some people will have been inconvenienced as they will have been forced to accept the consequences of their "choices" and actions. I speak as one who married a seventeen-year-old girl who was pregnant, and I do not admit that proudly. But I do say proudly that I chose *not* to take the "easier" way out, which was available.

Under the circumstances, if I am to err on this issue, I much prefer that it be on the conservative side. I am simply more comfortable with the consequences of a pro-life stand, even if science can one day prove that a fetus is, indeed and in fact, not a human being, which, at this point, seems highly unlikely given the direction scientific research has moved our knowledge. In other words, I prefer to answer for inconveniencing people rather than for killing them.

I suppose I must also address the "exceptions" issue, the three exceptions, of course, being when the pregnancy threatens the life of the mother or when pregnancy occurs as a result of rape or incest. I do not consider "the life of the mother" exception to be one that need be discussed because the issue of whether or not to terminate a pregnancy when the life of the mother is threatened is a medical decision which must rest with the doctor and the family and not a political issue to be resolved by the bickering of special-interest groups.

As for the other two "exceptions," rape and incest, I should point out that I was a volunteer counselor at the Lafayette Parish Rape Crisis Center for two years, and I still sit on the Board of Directors of the Rape Crisis Foundation. While I was a counselor, I served as an "escort," a counselor who actually met victims at the hospital and helped them through the initial trauma while the doctors and nurses gathered the physical evidence for the police. Several times when I was called out, the victims were children. The youngest victim I ever encountered was a six-year-old boy. My experiences as a rape and sexual-assault counselor were rewarding in that I had the knowledge that I was helping alleviate human suffering, but those experiences were also incredibly draining because to touch one who is in pain with the intent of relieving at least some of that pain means feeling, to a lesser degree, that pain yourself. So I bend my knee to no one when it comes to compassion for victims of sexual assault, but the point is that while I am deeply concerned and involved in attempting to deal with the issue of rape and sexual assault, the incidence of pregnancy as a consequence of a sexual attack is statistically insignificant—in fact, almost non-existent. Since the *Roe v. Wade* decision, abortion has come to be used simply as retroactive birth control, and I think we should be honest about that fact. In those very few instances where pregnancy does occur as a result of a sexual attack, I find myself still on the right-to-life side for the simple reason that, again, if an unborn fetus is a human being, why should that individual be made to suffer for the sins of another? I freely admit, however, that I find this final position an uncomfortable and troubling one.

It has also always seemed to me that the pro-abortion genderists let men off too easily. The availability of cheap, legal abortions and the position that it is simply a "woman's choice" is an argument for allowing men to act irresponsibly with impunity. Women, after all, still cannot impregnate themselves or each other, at least not yet. So, it stands to reason that the presence of a fetus presupposes a "choice" by a man also. Why let them off so easy? Perhaps that is why Professor Christina Sommers has written that some of their positions "make gender feminists . . . oddly unsympathetic to the women whom they claim to represent" (*New York Magazine*, 21 January 1991, p. 38).

Pro-abortion genderists also advance the argument that, without safe, affordable, legal abortion, there would be many more abused children in the world, as though abortion has solved or can solve the problem of child abuse in our society. Besides, who is it among us who can predict the quality of someone's life who is yet unborn. One of my favorite anecdotes on this subject is about an OB-GYN doctor who was a professor in a medical school, and one day he wrote on the board a list of genetic deficiencies from which a fetus was suffering. He asked the class to come up with a prognosis and a recommendation for the hypothetical pregnant patient. The students debated the issue for the entire period and finally told the professor that it would be their recommendation to the patient that she terminate the pregnancy. "Congratulations, class," the professor said, "you have just aborted Beethoven."

The politically correct genderists, however, refuse to deal with any of these points. The issue of abortion is a political one for them, pure and simple, and the issue revolves around "male dominance" of women in the "sex/gender system" around which our Western society is organized. "And since most of Western culture, according to this view, has been a testament to male power and transcendence, it is a moral evil dedicated to the enslavement of women and must be discarded" (*New York Magazine*, 21 January 1991, p. 38). In order to accomplish this goal, traditional sexual identities must be done away with, destroyed, or should I say, "deconstructed"? Remember deconstruction? Observe.

Alison Jaggar, a professor at the University of Cincinnati and the head of the American Philosophical Association's Committee on the Status of Women in Philosophy, maintains, that a simple candlelight dinner is "prostitution," not a *form* of prostitution, but the thing itself. Professor Jaggar admits that "both man and woman might be outraged" by such a description, "but the radical feminist argues this outrage is simply due to the participants' failure to perceive the social context in which the dinner occurs" (*New York Magazine*, 21 January 1991, p. 38).

Along similar lines, Andrea Parrot, a professor at Cornell, maintains that "any sexual intercourse without mutual desire is a form of rape" (*New York Magazine*, p. 39). Notice that Professor Parrot did not say "mutual *consent*," but "mutual *desire*." What this means, of course, is that "a woman is being raped if she has sex when not in the mood, even if she fails to inform her partner of that fact" (*New York Magazine*, p. 39). Furthermore, "rape is no longer limited to actual intercourse." In fact, according to a training manual at Swarthmore College, "acquaintance rape . . . spans a spectrum of incidents and behaviors ranging from crimes legally defined as rape to verbal harassment and inappropriate innuendo" (*New York Magazine*, 21 January 1991, p. 39).

As I have already pointed out, I am very sensitive to the issue of rape and sexual assault, but some of these positions are just too extreme for any rational person to accept. Before the impact of this kind of thinking is dismissed too quickly, however, remember the Clarence Thomas/Anita Hill soap opera.

The gender feminists even attack analytical thinking as part of male domination and compare scientific investigation to "the rape of nature." "A project sponsored by the state of New Jersey to integrate these views into college campuses has issued a set of 'feminist scholarship guidelines' that declares 'mind was male. Nature was female, and knowledge was created as an act of aggression—a passive nature had to be interrogated, unclothed, pen-etrated, and compelled by man to reveal her secrets'" (*New York Magazine*, 21 January 1991, p. 38).

The genderists who push these kinds of positions often quote Simone de Beauvoir who said, "No woman should be authorized to stay at home and raise children... precisely because if there is such a choice, too many women will make that one." It seems that these genderists are pro-choice only so long as *they* approve of the choice, once again revealing the hypocrisy so deeply rooted in PC thinking.

Speaking as a single parent who spent most of my time at home raising the three children from my first marriage when they were little, I say categorically that there is no job more demanding than raising children and taking care of a home. In those days when I had to be home so much with my little ones, going to work was a break. Let me also say, again speaking from experience, that I have a deep and abiding reverence for those people who stay home and raise America's children and do it well. Unfortunately, financial pressures do not always make that possible for today's family, and we must come to terms with the fact that America pays a price for every child whose mother cannot afford to stay at home because there is simply no way that anyone can work full time and still have the time or energy that young children demand. But, the PC genderists not only have no sympathy for those women who *must* work when they would prefer to be at home with their kids, they also, as Simone de Beauvoir's comment indicates, demean those women who are fortunate enough to be able to choose to stay at home and raise their children. This simply reveals the self-righteous arrogance of the PC crowd.

Nevertheless, the gender feminists predictably see the traditional family as "a cornerstone of women's oppression and would like to abolish the family altogether," which "imposes the prevailing masculine and feminine character structures on the next generation" and "enforces heterosexuality," and, of course, as you might expect, "heterosexuality [along with the family] is responsible for the subjugation of women" (*New York Magazine*, 21 January 1991, p. 38). According to Dinesh D'Souza's 1991 book, *Illiberal Education*, an instructor in a women's studies course at the University of Washington at Seattle asserted "on the first day of class . . . that 'the traditional American family represents a dysfunctional family unit'" (*Illiberal Education*, p. 202).

Next comes the inevitable PC gender-feminist move to homosexuality and lesbianism. According to the *Chronicle of Higher Education*, "the work [in the field of gay and lesbian studies] is closely connected to other developments in the humanities, broadly grouped under the category of cultural studies [aka: multiculturalism; aka: political correctness]. . . . The influence of various literary and cultural theories—especially feminism and Marxism—is relevant, as well. Lesbian studies, in particular, are deeply related to the growth of women's studies in the last 15 years" (*Chronicle*, 24 October 1990, p. A-4). This aspect of the politically correct movement manifests itself in two ways on college campuses.

The first is in selection of reading materials for students, so we are back to a consideration of the curriculum and the "canon." Catharine Stimpson, dean of the graduate school at Rutgers, for instance, has declared that her "ideal curriculum" would contain the book *Stars in My Pocket Like Grains of Sand*. Of this book, Dean Stimpson wrote, "Like many contemporary speculative fictions, *Stars in My Pocket* finds conventional heterosexuality absurd. The central characters are two men, Rat Korga and Marq Dyeth, who have a complex but ecstatic affair" (*New York Magazine*, 21 January 1991, p. 36).

The politically correct genderist move to eliminate sexual identity also manifests itself in the scholarship produced by these professors. Eve Kosofsky Sedgwick, a professor of English at Duke, who established her reputation with "a 1985 book on male bonding in 19th-century

English literature" entitled *Between Men: English Litera-*
ture and Male Homosocial Desire, is married but says she
"won't sue for libel" if she's identified as gay, though she
prefers the term "queer." Professor Sedgwick maintains,
"There is no aspect of 20th-century thought and culture
that can be understood well without asking how it's in-
tersected with issues of homosexual/heterosexual definition." She also says, "I'm not a gay man, but I feel as though
a lot of things about me, including my sexuality, are
enhanced by the visible and affirmative gay culture"
(*Chronicle*, 24 October 1990, p. A-4).

Professor Sedgwick is also the author of such papers
as "Jane Austen and the Masturbating Girl" and "How To
Bring Your Kids Up Gay" and a new book entitled *Epis-*
temology of the Closet. This book "makes an audacious
claim: Questions of sexual definition are at the heart of
all 20th-century thought and culture. Extending the work
of feminist scholars, Ms. Sedgwick argues that literature
should be analyzed through the lens of sexuality, adding
to the rubric of race, class, and gender [i.e., the PC isms]
popular in the humanities" (*Chronicle*, 24 October 1991,
p. A-4). Her book rests on the scholarship of the late
French philosopher Michel Foucault, who, in his book *The*
History of Sexuality, "argued that sexuality is 'socially
constructed' and has had varied meanings and purposes
throughout Western history." Professor Sedgwick's book
moves in the same direction and, according to a review
in the *Chronicle*, "with its insistence on identifying
dichotomies in the language used to describe sexual choice
. . . clearly aims to deconstruct." See? I told you—
deconstruction. Ultimately, through her work which some
have called "gay theory," "Ms. Sedgwick and others intend
to do more than read authors who identify themselves as
homosexual. Rather, she wants to question and 'destabi-
lize' the categories by which sexuality is defined"
(*Chronicle*, 24 October 1990, p. A-6).

Wayne Koestenbaum, assistant professor of English
at Yale University, said of Professor Sedgwick, "She is

the first person to really synthesize sophisticated critical work of the sort that takes in Marxism, feminism, and continental theory with an explicitly gay-positive tone" (*Chronicle*, 24 October 1991, p. A-6). Martha Vicinus, professor of English and Women's Studies at the University of Michigan and coauthor of *Hidden from History: Reclaiming the Gay and Lesbian Past*, adds, "Her work has helped move some of the debates on the suppressed homoerotic in literature to center stage" (p. A-6). Shelton Waldrep, a graduate student at Duke who is scheduled to teach a freshman seminar on gay-male fiction in 1992, says of Ms. Sedgwick, "She is a refuge. Gay and lesbian studies still needs institutional protection, and she knows how to provide that" (p. A-6). Professor Sedgwick is described by one colleague at Duke "as 'part mascot, part earth mother' to the gay-and-lesbian studies movement that is gaining momentum in some pockets of academe" (p. A-4).

Gaining momentum, indeed—in 1990, a gay and lesbian faculty research group at the University of California at Santa Cruz organized a conference called "Queer Theory." Teresa de Lauretis, a professor of the history of consciousness at Santa Cruz, said the goal was "to understand homosexuality not as a perversion or an inversion of normal sexual identity but as a sexual behavior and an identity on its own terms—as a cultural form in its own right" (*Chronicle*, 24 October 1990, p. A-6). In October of 1990, the fourth annual Lesbian, Bisexual, and Gay Studies Conference was held at Harvard. The conference, which featured over two hundred papers and eight hundred participants, "was organized under the title 'Pleasure/ Politics,' [and] spanned the spectrum, with a particular emphasis on how sexuality relates to race and nationality [multiculturalism]. Sessions addressed AIDS and the politics of fiction; lesbian pornography; homosexual marriages, past, present, and future; and matters of censorship" (p. A-6). There were also discussions of the relationships between gay and lesbian studies and women's studies.

Study groups in the area of gay and lesbian studies for faculty members and graduate students now meet regularly at Yale. In 1989, the first Department of Gay and Lesbian Studies was created at the City College of San Francisco, and in the spring of 1991, City University of New York opened its new Center for Lesbian and Gay Studies, "which will focus on research, curriculum development, and, eventually offer degrees" (*Chronicle*, 24 October 1990, p. A-4).

Richard D. Mohr, professor of philosophy at the University of Illinois at Urbana-Champaign says, "It's exploding; it's incredible the number of academic writing projects being born." Professor Mohr is the general editor of a new book series, the first three volumes of which are on gay male theater, homoerotic photography, and lesbian literary theory. The series is being published by Columbia University Press, and the first three volumes were issued this past year. Finally, David M. Halperin boldly proclaims that, "Gay and lesbian studies can do for sex what feminism did for gender" (*Chronicle*, 24 October 1990, p. A-4). I can hardly wait! But just what is it that the PC genderists want to "do for sex?" My wife had an experience that might give some insight into this part of the PC agenda.

When she was an undergraduate, my wife was pursued by a Ph.D. student, a lesbian, who had taken a fancy to her. Although my wife kept telling the lesbian person that she (my wife) was heterosexual and not interested in her (the lesbian person) in "that way," the lesbian person persisted. The lesbian person even started going to class with my wife, now, not just walking with her to class; the lesbian person was going *into* the classes with my wife and sitting next to her through the class. These were classes in which the lesbian person was not enrolled because, as already mentioned, my wife was just an undergraduate (a sophomore), and the lesbian person was a Ph.D. student. Finally, one of my wife's professors, thinking that the lesbian person was with my wife, stopped her (my wife) and asked her what a Ph.D. student was doing in an undergraduate class. At that point, my wife broke down, started crying, and told the professor what had been going on. The professor went to the graduate director, and my wife was finally left alone.

This episode reveals two things. First of all, it shows just how aggressive and persistent some of these people can be. I suggest that if a man did to a woman what the lesbian person did to my wife, the PC genderists would want him castrated for sexual harassment. Remember Anita Hill? More PC hypocrisy.

Secondly, and perhaps more importantly, some of the things the lesbian person said to my wife give a pretty clear insight into the agenda of the PC genderists. Throughout the period of harassment, the lesbian person kept saying things to my wife like, "You're much too intelligent and sensitive to just be straight." The implication of this statement is that homosexuality is associated with a higher level of intelligence and sensitivity than heterosexuality. So the ultimate aim of the PC genderists is not merely to present homosexuality on an equal footing, so to speak, with heterosexuality; the goal is to elevate homosexuality *above* heterosexuality. In other words, if you're not *at least* bisexual, it's because you're not intelligent enough or sensitive enough or because you're homophobic, i.e., as already mentioned, there's something *wrong* with *you*. Get it? Well, if that is what the PC genderists want to "do for sex," my response is, "Thanks, but no thanks. I like my sex just the way it is, just me and my wife." But my wife and I, of course, are a traditional couple in a traditional family unit, which, according to the genderists, "imposes the prevailing masculine and feminine character structures on the next generation [our kids]" and "enforces heterosexuality." This, according to the PC genderists, is very PNC, a "dysfunctional family unit." What the PC genderists envision is "a society where . . . one woman could inseminate another, men could lactate, and fertilized ova could be transferred into women's or even men's bodies" (*New York Magazine*, 21 January 1991, p. 38).

Such statements reveal two gaping holes in the logic of this PC "ism." First of all, one might ask just how the genderists would realize the aforementioned "vision" when they have attacked and rejected scientific investigation as "the rape of nature." I suggest that accomplishing the things articulated in their "vision" would take some *serious, new* technologies which would require scientific research which the PC genderists claim is part of the Western tradition of "male dominance."

The second problem with the PC genderist "vision" is articulated by Kay Ebeling, who lives in Humboldt, California, and is a single mother with a two-year-old daughter and an axe to grind. She is a freelance writer, and she wrote a piece that was published in the opinion section of the 19 November 1990 issue of *Newsweek*. The title of her piece was "The Failure of Feminism." Here are some excerpts:

> To me, feminism has backfired against women. In 1973 I left what could have been a perfectly good marriage, taking with me a child in diapers, a 10-year-old Plymouth and Volume 1, Number One of *Ms*. Magazine. I was convinced I could make it on my own. In the last 15 years my ex has married or lived with a succession of women. As he gets older, his women stay in their 20's. Meanwhile, I've stayed unattached. He drives a BMW. I ride buses.
>
> Today I see feminism as the Great Experiment That Failed, and women in my generation, its perpetrators, are the casualties. . . . Feminism freed men, not women.
>
> The main message of feminism was: woman, you don't need a man; . . . it was a philosophy that made divorce and cohabitation casual and routine. Feminism made women disposable. So today a lot of females are around 40 and single with a couple of kids to raise on their own. . . . Feminism gave men all the financial and personal advantages over women.
>
> What's worse, we asked for it. Many women decided: you don't need a family structure to raise

your children. We packed them off to day-care
centers . . . put on our suits and ties, packed our
briefcases . . . convinced that there was no difference
between ourselves and the guys in the other offices.
. . .

   How wrong we were. Because like it or not,
women have babies. It's this biological thing that's
just there, these organs we're born with. The truth
is, a woman can't live the true feminist life unless
she denies her child-bearing biology. . . .
   The reality of feminism is a lot of frenzied and
overworked women dropping kids off at day-care
centers.

The gender feminists would have Ms. Ebeling for
lunch, and you too if you agreed with anything she said.
Talk about PNC. What Ms. Ebeling points out is yet another
instance of PC running headfirst into scientific fact, the
simple fact that men and women are *different*, fundamentally and forever different, physically and emotionally
different. This is a physiological fact, not a sexist argument.
I, for one, am terribly thankful for this difference. The PC
police will have an APB out on me for that. And since
the PC police are gonna get us anyway, let's really live
dangerously and consider for a moment if it might just be
possible that "the traditional family unit," which is based
on "the prevailing masculine and feminine structures," is
actually nothing more than a concession to what Ms.
Ebeling calls "this biological thing," you know—that troubling little PNC fact that women have babies and men
don't. But not to be deterred by little things like glaring
contradictions or biological reality, the PC genderists are
pushing forward to hasten the deconstruction of traditional
"masculine and feminine structures" and sexual identities.
   As with all other aspects of the PC movement, this
particular "ism" has not confined itself to the university
campus. Professor Eve Sedgwick got involved in the Senate
race in North Carolina in 1990, and "her pocketbook
sport[ed] a fluorescent orange sticker: 'Another Queer

Against Helms.' She and some of her students are [also] involved in a local chapter of ACT-UP!, the AIDS activist organization" (*Chronicle*, 24 October 1990, p. A-6). A member of this organization makes a cameo appearance in a recent film entitled *Jesus Christ Condom,* which debuted at the Third Annual New York International Festival of Gay and Lesbian Films. The film features an AIDS activist dressed as the traditional Jesus and wearing a crown of thorns. Standing on the steps of St. Patrick's Cathedral, the character delivers a half hour diatribe against Christianity and finally denounces Cardinal O'Connor, who has opposed the PC position of free distribution of condoms in public schools. During his oration, the character portraying Jesus says, "My mom [Mary] was a virgin and boy did she miss out." He then takes out a condom and says, "Make sure your second *cumming* [my italics] is a safe one. Use condoms." Then the member of ACT-UP! crumbles communion wafers on the floor and stomps on them ("Tax Revolting," *New York Guardian*, July 1991).

If you find this offensive, you are most certainly PNC and homophobic, but, hold on; *you also paid for this film.* That's right, folks; I just described a film that was yet another project funded with your tax money through the National Endowment for the Arts (the N.E.A.). Other N.E.A. funded projects include a "play" in which the actor comes on stage carrying a toilet and a Bible. The "actor" proceeds to tear pages out of the Bible and toss them into the toilet while urinating into it. Impressed? You paid for it. The 1991 San Francisco International Lesbian and Gay Film Festival was also funded for the fourth straight year with an N.E.A. grant. According to an article entitled "Tax Revolting," which appeared in the July 1991 issue of *The New York Guardian*, the N.E.A. also awarded a grant to the Alice B. Theater Company in Seattle "to help support the production of several homosexual plays, one of which, *Lust and Pity*, is described as a 'dark comedy about lesbians who wear lipstick and very little else'." And I missed it! Darn! And let us not forget the infamous Mapplethorpe exhibit which had a strongly homoerotic message and which featured photographs of naked children, and the even more famous "Piss Christ," a five foot by three foot photograph of a crucifix submerged in a jar of urine, also funded by an N.E.A. grant.

Such displays of "art" always bring to mind a movie I saw many years ago entitled *Butterflies Are Free*. It was a warm and tender story of a blind guy trying to live on his own in New York City whose mother would not leave him alone simply because she is so concerned about him. She finally finds the love to let her son go, but there is a scene in the movie in which the mother is having a conversation with the director of a play which is being produced in the Village. The director is going on and on about the play which includes nudity and sex on stage. When he sees that the woman is disapproving, he says, "These things are a part of life." She responds, "So is diarrhea, but I wouldn't classify that as entertainment either."

Senator Jesse Helms of North Carolina, of course, has been the most vocal critic of the use of federal tax dollars to fund "art" of the kind previously described, which would explain Professor Sedgwick's "fluorescent orange sticker." I'll never forget the discussion we had in the faculty lounge when the media was really pushing the censorship issue using the Mapplethorpe exhibit as an example. Some of my colleagues were, of course, beating up on Jesse Helms and accusing him (and me because I happened to agree with him) of playing the role of censor. I will not go into my argument against censorship because I would not presume to outdo Milton, whose *Areopagitica* is the definitive word on the subject. Let me simply state categorically, as I did that day in the lounge, that I would not ban the production of such "art," even though I do find it extremely offensive. But I also say that if "artists" find it necessary to express themselves in such a manner, let them pay for it themselves or find patrons to provide private funding for it, the way *real* artists used to because I do reserve my right as a taxpayer not to pay for things which I consider to be pornographic and obscene. Guess what came next. One of my colleagues asked, "Ah, but what *is* obscene?"

"Look it up," I said.

Ironically, when Anita Hill was accusing Clarence Thomas of describing scenes from "pornographic" movies and making other "obscene" comments, not *one* of my colleagues seemed to have any problem knowing exactly what Ms. Hill was talking about. In other words, in the context of the Thomas/Hill soap opera, "pornographic" and "obscene" suddenly became words whose definitions were very clear. Again, there's that fundamental hypocrisy. Nevertheless, the amount of federal funding being provided to spread the PC message concerning genderism and homosexuality is sobering and indicates just how active and strong such groups are becoming off campus as well as on. They're even getting international!

The University of Calgary in Canada, publicly supported, sponsored the art exhibit *The Castration of St. Paul.* "The exhibit was created by a 'post-Christian feminist collective' of anonymous Calgary art students as an expression of their view of Christianity's patriarchal nature. It featured thirty photographs of male genitals, each labeled with the name of a Biblical figure or Christian saint." The display was "praised" by the head of the art department for its "humor" (*Citizen*, 21 October 1991, p. 15).

Perhaps the most radical gay-lesbian activist organization is "Queer Nation." One of the national officers of Queer Nation was interviewed on a national news broadcast recently, and she said, "I want to be present at the death of the first gay basher so that I can open his skull with my machete and spread his brains all over the walls of the *New York Times.*" This whole notion of "gay-bashing" is also intriguing. Frank Acqueno, a gay freelance writer who made an appearance on a recent "Donahue" show, made a comment which indicates how quickly PC homosexuals and genderists are to jump to this as an issue.

When people in the audience took issue with some of the things he said, Mr. Acqueno said that "no one had the right to beat [him] up just because [he] was gay." Now this comment was totally unrelated to what was being discussed at the time, but in keeping with this PC penchant for name-calling, if you take issue with anything a homosexual says or even discuss homosexuality in anything other than PC terms, you will finally be called a homophobe or a gay basher or both. Now a gay basher is someone who physically beats up gay people, and PC gay rights activists want this treated legally as a specific crime. This is yet another indication that homosexuals consider themselves as better than other people and are demanding not equality but special consideration for themselves. In other words, according to PC homosexuals and genderists, beating up a gay person is a more serious crime than beating up a straight person. I find this to be as offensive as it is illogical. Assault and battery is against the law, period. If you physically assault *anyone* for *any* reason, you can and should be prosecuted, and the race, creed, national origin, sex, or sexual orientation and/or preference of your victim is not and should not be relevant. It is *only* when laws are applied equally that justice is truly served. But, again, these PC persons are not interested in equality or justice.

Nevertheless, I am as offended by gay bashing as I am by Queer Nation. This group has staged huge demonstrations featuring marches with chants such as, "We're here! We're queer! Get used to it!" They have also staged "deep kissing" demonstrations in public. The purpose of all this, of course, is to force American society to confront its "homophobia." Notice the PC penchant for *ad hominem* logic. If you do not accept the PC position on homosexuality, there is something *wrong* with you; i.e., you suffer from a "phobia," which is defined as "an irrational, illogical, excessive, exaggerated, morbid, or persistent fear." On his recent program dealing with the controversy over whether homosexuals are born that way or whether they choose that life-style, Phil Donahue called homophobia a "dis-

ease." I guess he knows, but I didn't know Phil Donahue
went to medical school. Once again, there is simply no
way to take issue with any PC position without being
attacked and insulted in such a way, which is an interesting
way of promoting discussion.

     I, for instance, would be considered homophobic by
the PC crowd because I would take the position that sexual
acts "performed" in public cheapen the act and the actors.
To me, what makes sex beautiful and wonderful is intimacy, which means (deconstruction notwithstanding) that
you don't do it in public, not to mention the fact that such
intimacy also separates human beings from dogs and cats
in alleys and fields. When I am forced to witness a sexual
act *of any kind*, those engaged in the act become exhibi-
tionists and I am victimized by being turned into a voyeur
against my will. Jimmy Swaggart is, of course, used by
the PC crowd as a clear and obvious example of perversion,
yet, their public displays have the effect of turning *everyone*
into Jimmy Swaggart. More PC hypocrisy.

     Furthermore, suppose there is a "rational" explanation
for most people's aversion to homosexuality? That explanation might be that an aversion to homosexuality is a
response to the deepest instinct any animal has, i.e., the
instinct to survive. Homosexuality is, after all, ultimately,
a threat to the survival of the human species because if
everyone were homosexual, humankind would cease to
exist because without heterosexual activity, you can't pro-
create. That's logical, isn't it? But who cares? It's PNC!
It's homophobic! So what? Let's push the envelope.
Suppose I were to say that I find homosexuals who are
intent upon making their sexuality a public issue to be some
of the most paranoid people I have ever encountered, and
I suggest that what they call "homophobia" is nothing but
a classic case of their projection of their paranoia onto
heterosexuals. Boy, the PC police are really gonna get me
for that one. But I don't care; I have tenure!

     If such discussions were allowed, and a PC person
were to reject my previous point on the aversion to

homosexuality being a response to the instinct to survive on the basis that human beings are not just animals and that one's being is more than just a physical body, then, according to that logic (with which I agree) one's sex and/or sexual preference and/or sexual orientation simply isn't an issue; so why bring it up in the first place? I will boldly proclaim that I do have friends and colleagues who are homosexual. I sit with them, talk with them, laugh with them, and socialize with them, not because I am such a liberal, but because they do not make their sexuality an issue. My heterosexual friends don't discuss their sex lives with me, why should my homosexual friends do so? You must remember that not all liberals are PC. In fact, as I pointed out in chapter 1, many of my colleagues who are certainly *not* conservative find PC as ridiculous as I do.

I believe that all my friends (and everyone else for that matter) have an absolute right to do with consenting adults whatever they please in the privacy of their homes and especially in their own bedrooms, and I'll defend those rights to the death. But, you remember, I'm into that intimacy thing. Furthermore, as long as they don't ask my opinion about what they do, it's none of my business. But when homosexuals try to shove their life-style down "straight" people's throats (no pun intended) and to make their sexual preference and/or orientation a public issue and demand special treatment for it, then they had better be ready to stand for the public's reaction. These kinds of positions, however, promote serious consideration and open discussion of the issues, and the PC crowd prefers to simply dismiss me and my points as examples of "homophobia." People who think this way are simply not interested in discussing anything seriously, and a recent "Donahue" program revealed that one reason for that just might be that these PC folks may well be intelligent enough to understand that when they try to discuss these matters in a serious way, it becomes clear how contradictory and intellectually fraudulent all this PC business really is.

As already mentioned, Phil Donahue did a show on

some of the recent discoveries in sexual studies which tend
to indicate that there may be a genetic factor in homosexuality. There has been quite a bit of research in this area
of late, and Donahue had a scientist on his show who had
just completed and published the results of such a study
and who has become very controversial. Dr. Simon Levay
of the Salk Institute conducted a study of the brains of
heterosexual and homosexual males. What he found was
that the hypothalamus, the part of the brain which forms
the floor of the third ventricle and regulates many basic
body functions (including sexual), was consistently and
significantly larger in the brains of heterosexual males. Dr.
Levay said, "My results suggest that there are deep, biological differences between gay and straight men which
probably come about in the womb when the brain is putting
itself together. In other words, gay men or straight men
are born that way rather than choosing to be gay or straight."

There are, however, people who are up in arms over
Dr. Levay's research and his conclusions. Mr. Donahue
commented that, "This type of research is very much
contaminated by the disease of homophobia, but it does
not follow that because there's prejudice out there that we
shouldn't study this." I found myself feeling a little uncomfortable at this point because I agreed with Donahue.

James Weinrich, a Ph.D. in evolutionary biology and
author of the book *Sexual Landscapes*, who was also a guest
on the show, applauded Dr. Levay's work and also agreed
with Donahue that we should press forward with such
research. "We would not have been able to fight AIDS
biologically if we had not had hundreds of millions of
dollars spent on basic research about how viruses work.
We are crippled in the fight against AIDS today because
we have not been able to spend hundred of millions of
dollars on sex research to understand why it is that people
do what they do in bed."

Now you might conclude based on the previous comments that those who oppose Dr. Levay's research are
"straight," right-wing, conservative Republicans, who

everybody knows are the most "homophobic" people there are. Right? Wrong! The men on Donahue's show who were there to speak against Dr. Levay and his work were homosexuals! John P. de Cecco, a professor of psychology at San Francisco State and editor of *The Journal of Homosexuality* insisted, "This research has a political agenda, and it's *not* to make people freer about sex. . . . He [Levay] is making a political assertion about the causes of people's sexual preference based on his personal feelings, . . . but it's being couched in the language of science. It's not science."

Mr. Donahue said, "But you're asking us to accept your diagnosis of Dr. Levay's motivation."

Professor de Cecco responded, "Dr. Levay made the public statement here in New York at a symposium at the Graduate Center of City University of New York, and he said, 'I was very happy to find what I found.'"

Dr. Levay said, "Yes, I was."

Dr. Weinrich came to Dr. Levay's defense and said, "Any scientist is happy to find a statistically significant finding. That gets you tenure."

Frank Aqueno, the previously mentioned gay freelance writer and performing artist, was also on the show to maintain that homosexuality was not genetic but a choice; a "rational" choice, he called it. Mr. Aqueno maintained, "When I was five or four or three, I was absorbing the society around me, and I noticed when I was growing up that women were not my equals. That was absorbed. I couldn't talk about it. I couldn't speak about it. I didn't have the words for it, but I observed it. I saw it. I don't approve of it, but that's the world I was born into. Later on when the juices started flowing and I started to have [sexual] fantasies, they were about men because they were my equals."

Dr. Levay called that "the most ridiculous" thing he'd ever heard. He then said, "The deepest feelings you have within yourself about who you most prefer to have sex with, that's something you have no choice about."

"That's wrong; that's simply wrong," Mr. Aqueno insisted.

Dotson Rader, who is also a gay freelance writer, was also a guest on the show and there to speak against Dr. Levay. Mr. Rader said, "I think it [homosexuality] is volitional. Most gay men I know have had sex with women. It's not that they're incapable of having sex with women; it's that they prefer and are more comfortable having sex with men. And I personally think this research [Dr. Levay's] is fascistic. By asking the question, what causes homosexuality, you're showing a bias and it's homophobic."

I found all this confusing because I understood that it was homosexuals themselves who had come up with the notion that homosexuality was an "orientation" rather than a "preference," therefore, it wasn't something to be moralized about. But the homosexuals on Donahue's show were not only maintaining that homosexuality was a "choice," a conscious "preference," they were accusing Dr. Levay's research of being homophobic. But to confuse matters even more, Dr. Levay, himself, is a homosexual as well! In fact, he said that it was when his lover died of AIDS that he became interested in doing the research.

So let's see if we've got this straight, no pun intended. We've got a homosexual scientist at the Salk Institute doing research to determine whether or not there is a genetic component in homosexuality, which would validate the position originally taken by the gay community that homosexuality is a matter of "orientation" rather than "preference," and the homosexuals are calling his research homophobic. And the homosexual scientists say that those who speak out against their research are homophobic and are getting in the way of possibly finding a cure for AIDS. Got it? In other words, the homosexuals are calling each other homophobic and blaming each other for there not being a cure for AIDS when all that used to be Ronald Reagan's fault. Talk about getting careless with your name-calling.

Nevertheless, Mr. Rader went on to maintain that the

question of whether someone is born gay or chooses to be gay is "unanswerable," and that "if you develop conclusively that there is some sort of gene that causes a predilection to homosexuality, you're going to have these bone-headed fundamentalists coming up and saying, 'Let's do research on how to change the genetic nature of these fetuses or let's abort them.'"

A lady in the audience responded to Mr. Rader by saying, "I'm a 'bone-headed fundamentalist,' and I don't believe in abortion."

When another lady in the audience voiced an objection to the insulting manner in which the homosexuals on the show kept referring to the "fundamentalist yahoos," Mr. Donahue said, "I don't think anybody said 'fundamentalist yahoos' with a respectful bow to what is generally described as the conservative, Christian community. We would not want to call them yahoos."

His obvious sarcasm notwithstanding, Donahue was right. No one had referred to the conservative, Christian community as "fundamentalist yahoos." His homosexual guests were much more brutal than that. They called them "bone-headed fundamentalists," and "stupid bigots." Interestingly enough, Dr. Levay was the only one who was never abusive of conservatives or Christians during the show.

Nevertheless, at one point in the program, Mr. Acqueno was attempting to explain the nature of the "choice" to be homosexual. "It's not like choosing meat or potatoes," he said. Then he asked the question, "Do you remember *choosing* to walk?" Now, did I miss something? The man who was arguing that homosexuality was a "rational choice" then compared it to "choosing to walk." Call me dense, but I figure he just contradicted himself.

Mr. Rader, who called Dr. Levay's research "fascistic" and "homophobic," also said that asking what causes homosexuality is "like asking what causes blue eyes instead of brown eyes." Again, call me dense, but in making that statement, didn't this guy, who claimed that homosexuality was "volitional," just compare it to a genetic trait? But that's the beauty of deconstruction; it lets you do that because, as with PC history, being "objective" and "definitive" is abandoned for the sake of being "interesting and suggestive" and for the sake of "political agendas." In other words, scientific fact goes the way of historical fact, and everything is reduced to a mere matter of opinion, and all opinions are equal, and this is what makes this whole PC business a colossal example of intellectual fraud.

As I have already pointed out, all opinions are most certainly *not* created equal. There is a substantive and significant difference between informed opinions and uninformed opinions, and any mode of thinking which does not recognize or denies this elementary observation runs afoul of all categories of logical thought. In the final analysis, Mr. Rader and Mr. Acqueno do not even belong on the same stage with Dr. Levay. On the one hand, we have a scientist from one of the most prestigious institutes in the world simply sharing the results of his research. On the other hand, we have homosexuals saying they don't like what he's doing. The whole construct is absurd. While Mr. Rader and Mr. Acqueno are most certainly entitled to their opinions, they have no credentials whatsoever to make their opinions about Dr. Levay's work of any consequence to anyone who is interested in science. Even Professor de Cecco, while having more substantial academic credentials than the other two, is still out of his field and, therefore, really in no position to question Dr. Levay's work either. That is why Professor de Cecco engaged in the tactic so typical of the PC crowd and attacked Dr. Levay personally and raised questions about the motivation of the research rather than dealing with what Dr. Weinrich called the statistically significant findings of Dr. Levay's work. The simple fact is that, from a scientific point of view, Dr. Levay's motivations are irrelevant unless he somehow alters his results to suit his political agenda, and if that is what Professor de Cecco is accusing Dr. Levay of having done, he'd better be able to prove it because that is a very serious charge, indeed.

The only purely scientific objection Professor de Cecco raised was when he said that there had been other such studies done before, and the people who conducted the studies were never able to replicate the results. Now that would be a legitimate, scientific basis on which to challenge Levay's findings, but Levay responded to that by saying, "That's not true." Levay is right; de Cecco is wrong. Mr. Acqueno also kept complaining that there was no money for research in the psychological aspect of homosexuality to provide scientific evidence that it was, in fact, a matter of choice. Mr. Acqueno is wrong also. There is such research being done, and guess what the results suggest?

According to the 18 December 1991 issue of the *Chronicle of Higher Education*, J. Michael Bailey, an assistant professor of psychology at Northwestern University, and Richard C. Pillard, a professor of psychiatry at Boston University's medical school, have also looked into the possibility of a genetic component in homosexuality, and the results of their research were published in the December 1991 issue of the *Archives of General Psychiatry*. Their findings "strongly indicate" that there is, indeed, a genetic component to homosexuality; in other words, reinforcing Dr. Levay's results from a psychiatric vantage point. Frederick L. Whitam, a professor of sociology at Arizona State University "says a twins study that he recently concluded but has not yet published came up with results similar to those of Mr. Bailey and Dr. Pillard." (*Chronicle*, 5 Feb. 1992, p. A-7). Scientific study and fact, however, is no match for PC logic, and Professor Bailey was quoted in the 5 February 1992 issue of the *Chronicle* as saying, "I'm a little bit dismayed by some of the critical reaction in the gay community I get."

Donahue's program was actually amusing for two reasons. First of all, it featured people who had no scientific credentials attempting to engage in a scientific discussion, which is silly by any standard except deconstruction. In addition and as already mentioned, what was even more amusing was that his homosexual guests were calling each other homophobic. Like I said, it can get pretty ridiculous.

The program was also disturbing because, at one point in the show, Mr. Donahue said to Mr. Rader, "Your position is inhibiting inquiry."

Mr. Rader responded, "I *want* to inhibit inquiry because it's politically dangerous."

There was the first completely honest admission I have ever heard from the PC crowd that part of their agenda is to "inhibit inquiry." The reason that Mr. Rader would "inhibit inquiry" is because he is afraid of what he assumes some people might do with the knowledge that the inquiry might provide. The only problem is that, throughout human history, fear has always been the arch-enemy of efforts to expand human knowledge. Fear and intellectual curiosity, which leads to investigation and to discovery, have always been and will forever remain hopelessly at odds. Ironically, not only do Mr. Nader and his PC homosexual cohorts toss the term "homophobic" around like the McCarthyites tossed around the epithet "communist," it is important to keep in mind that a "phobia" is an irrational fear. Yet, Mr. Rader deliberately intends to "inhibit inquiry" because of *his* fear. Hypocrisy? I think so.

An interesting question would be exactly what it is that Mr. Rader and his PC homosexual cohorts are afraid of. Could it be that they are afraid that scientific research just might "establish conclusively," as Mr. Rader put it, that homosexuality is, in fact, a result of a genetic abnormality? Is that what they fear? Suppose medical science could "establish [this] conclusively?" Would Mr. Rader and his PC homosexual cohorts bury the research simply because it doesn't suit their political agenda? Let me say categorically that this little homophobe is not afraid of *any* scientific research in this or any other area, and, like a true scholar, I'm always willing to let the facts prove me wrong, and I challenge the PC genderists to show the same courage.

But they will never accept such a challenge because if facts are ever "established conclusively," which is the ultimate aim of pure research, you can't play deconstruction anymore. So long as the questions remain "unanswerable," which is Mr. Rader's final word on the subject, he and others of his ilk can stay on their logical merry-go-round, going 'round and 'round *ad infinitum*, defining and redefining their terms in any way they choose, even if they contradict themselves. And if you don't accept virtually *everything* they say on *their* terms, contradictions notwithstanding, then there is something *wrong* with *you*, i.e., homophobia. I must say that I don't blame these PC genderists for clinging so tenaciously to such a system. It's a perfect logical circle! Still, this is one little homophobe who will *not* be intimidated by the PC genderists, and it is important that they be confronted by someone because, like its brother/sister isms, politically correct genderism, has also found its way into the elementary and secondary school system in this country.

This PC "ism" surfaces in our public schools in the discussion of and controversy over sex education, which has become more heated with the advent of the AIDS crisis. The PC crowd, of course, argues for a sex education curriculum in public schools which pushes the notion of "safe sex." The PC crowd interprets "safe sex" to mean the use of a condom; therefore, central to the sex education curriculum they are pushing is free condom distribution in public schools.

This whole business about "safe sex" may well be the most pernicious lie yet spawned by the PC movement. Let us return to the beginning. C. Everett Koop, then Surgeon General of the United States, made a statement concerning AIDS and the spread of the HIV virus which started the whole thing. Dr. Koop said, to prevent contracting the AIDS virus, we must practice abstinence and monogamy. That sounds strangely like traditional family values, those things the PC crowd so despises. That notwithstanding, a study was done which revealed that high-school kids thought "monogamy" meant sleeping with one person at a time! Of course, from a deconstructive point of view, such a "definition" would be valid, but in this particular case, such deconstructive logic just might kill our kids. Nevertheless, Koop went on to say that barring abstinence and a monogamous relationship with an uninfected person, the use of a condom was the next best line of defense against contracting the HIV virus. Now please understand, Dr. Koop *never* said that the use of a condom made sex "safe." It was simply one method, an imperfect one and a distant third to the first two, to protect oneself. But the PC "safe sex" crowd created the misconception that using a condom *guaranteed* that one was "safe." The more accurate and appropriate phrase would have been and should have been "saf*er* sex," not "safe sex."

Those of us who oppose "sex education" in school do so because we are afraid of what our kids are going to be taught. I don't want my kids taught that homosexuality is an "acceptable, alternate life-style," or that using a condom will positively prevent AIDS or pregnancy, or that abortion is an acceptable option if one happens to get pregnant. And I don't care what any PC educator thinks of my positions. I will teach my kids what I think is right, and I ask permission of or offer apologies to no one. I also regard the PC position that our kids are going to be sexually active whether we like it or not as the greatest insult to our kids I have ever heard. Such a position presupposes that our kids today are totally incapable of behavior control, for moral or medical reasons, a notion I find absurd.

Along these lines, there was a minister who appeared on a "Donahue" program who had distributed condoms in his church. The minister actually said, "If Jesus were here today, he'd say to Mary [Magdeline], 'Now, Mary, you gotta stop this, but I know how you are, so, just in case, use this,' and he'd give her a condom." If I hadn't heard this with my own ears, I wouldn't believe it. Clearly PC thinking recognizes and respects no boundaries when it comes to rewriting history to suit its political agendas.

The simple fact is that kids are becoming more and more sexually active at earlier and earlier ages. And being "sexually active" does not merely mean that they lose their virginity as a result of careless behavior in a moment of passion. It means that they are graduating from high school having had sex on a regular basis with multiple partners. I have two teen-agers, and they have confirmed this to me, not that I needed them to. I graduated from high school in 1971 *as a virgin*, and I am certain that I was the rule and not the exception. How could things have changed so drastically so quickly? Are kids today so different from kids just twenty years ago? I don't think so. The fact is that telling kids that they're going to be sexually active anyway and that they just need to be "safe," i.e., use a condom, is not only giving them permission to behave in this manner, it has become a self-fulfilling prophecy. The staggering increases in teen sexual activity and teen pregnancy are facts which speak for themselves. But, again, the PC crowd never lets little things like facts stand in the way of its "agenda."

I was having a discussion concerning this matter one day in the faculty lounge with a colleague who was angry over the lack of sex education in public schools. I asked him at what age children should be introduced to this area. My colleague (who, interestingly enough, has no children) said as soon as they became sexually curious. My response was, while that did make sense, kids become "sexually curious," as he put it, at different ages. Sex education in public schools, however, would have to be introduced at a specific grade level which would presuppose that all kids become sexually curious at the same time and to the same extent, which, again, is simply not so.

I then asked my colleague what he would teach in sex education classes. He insisted that kids must be taught the facts about human reproduction. I said they learn that in biology class. I maintain that if the truth be told, sex education is nothing but an attempt by PC educators to indoctrinate young children on issues like homosexuality

and abortion. I further maintain that I would *not* object
to sex education if, indeed, it stuck to the "facts about
human reproduction" and AIDS and other sexually trans-
mitted diseases, because, again, the simple facts about
AIDS reinforce the traditional family values of abstinence
and monogamy which I am attempting to instill in my
children. "So," he said, "you think sex education should
be about scaring kids?" To my surprise and pleasure,
another colleague who was seated at the table responded,
"Yes, because the facts *are* scary." I was surprised because
I am usually alone in voicing such politically incorrect
positions. I was pleased because it appears that more and
more of my PNC colleagues in the professoriate are starting
to speak out against all this PC nonsense, and make no
mistake about the kind of courage this takes because the
PC crowd knows how to exact a cost from those who oppose
them.

Chapter 5

PC TERRORISM

As I have been pointing out, some of the aspects of the politically correct movement are so outlandish that they clearly cross the line from the sublime to the ridiculous. As mentioned in chapter 1, the PC movement has recently come to be parodied in comic strips. The movement was the subject of the nationally syndicated cartoon *Outland*, and that strip is included for your entertainment.

"The Campus Adventures of 'Politically Correct Person'" is also a regular feature in the *Brown Daily Herald*, the student newspaper at Brown University in Providence, Rhode Island. The comic strip was created by undergraduate cartoonist Jeff Shesol. Several of the strips are included for enjoyment.

The Campus Adventures of 'Politically Correct Person'

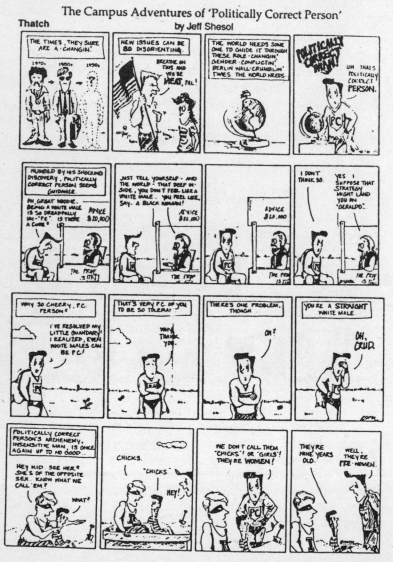

Politically correct sensitivity was also the subject of a satirical editorial by Joe Spear, a columnist for the Baton Rouge *Morning Advocate*. A few excerpts from Mr. Spear's piece are included for your consideration.

Need help choosing a name for your new business, club, athletic team? Having trouble picking out a politically correct costume for your next party?

Call us at 1-555-PCNONOS. We have a computer bank of over half a million words in 503 languages and 2,976 dialects that might hurt the feelings of somebody somewhere in the world.

Tom: Hello, is this the Clearinghouse for Politically Correct stuff?

PC Policeperson: Yes, how may I help you?

Tom: We're starting a badminton league here in Bay City and we want to call our team the Barracudas. Any problem?

PCP: A definite no-no. Barracuda is a word often applied to aggressive womyn. Stay away from it.

Dick: Hello, I'm in charge of the office Halloween party and we've got some people who want to come dressed as rocks. Your advice, please.

PCP: Oh heavens, no! Making fun of rocks offends geologists, petrologists and jewelers. Not to mention the use of the word in reference to scrota, which would constitute verbal sexism . . .

Harry: Yo, PCers, this is Harry, down in Houston, you know. I work in an S & L, see, and we want to name our softball team the Running Dogs of Capitalism. Any problem?

PCP: Forget it, Harry. Animals are the equivalent of humans and should not be turned into objects of ridicule. This constitutes speciesism. Dogs are people too, you know.

Joe: I'm calling about this Native American protest against the names of professional sports teams. They don't like it because Atlanta's team is called the Braves. They didn't like it when the fans did the Seminole chant. They didn't like the Tomahawk

chop. Even Jimmy Carter, Mr. Human Rights, said
Indians were being portrayed positively and no offense
should be taken. Where will it end? . . .

Where, indeed. The American Indian Movement
(A.I.M.) staged a major demonstration at the 1992 Superbowl
in Minnesota to protest the use of Indian (I mean Native
American) nicknames by professional sports teams and to
call for a stop to the practice. You realize, of course, that
the A.I.M. really needs to change its name because the one
it uses now is PNC. It should be called The Native American
Movement (N.A.M.). See? You just can't be too careful
these days. Were you aware that a recent edition of a major
dictionary listed *womyn* as an acceptable alternate spelling
for women? Seriously! That's to get the "men" out of
"women." Get it?

If you were amused by anything you just read, you
are definitely not politically correct, because of all the
things the PC movement claims as its own, one thing it
sorely lacks is a sense of humor, which is due to the
hyperbolic sensitivity of its proponents. I had a professor
once who said, "Never give anyone who has no sense of
humor the last word on anything." I have always found
that to be good advice. To the PC crowd, nothing is funny
about PC, and nothing is more indicative of a loss of
perspective than the lack of a sense of humor, which,
according to Mark Twain, would be the real unforgiveable
sin. But, satire, of course, uses humor to drive to the heart
of a very serious issue. Consider the following example.

Kiley Armstrong of the Associated Press wrote a piece
which was printed on the front page of a supplement to
the *Daily Advertiser* called "The Express Line." The piece
appeared in Volume I, Issue 27, 12-18 February 1992 and
was entitled "The PC Guide to Life in the 90s," which is
also the title of a new book. Here are some excerpts.

The question was asked, "What's your reaction to a
rock video featuring scantily clad women?"

(Decidedly the Wrong Answer: 'Awwwww right!!!!')

What's your view on military women in combat?

(Wrong Answer: 'They just want a legal excuse to kill men.')

These are actually excerpts from the book by Eric Lefcowitz who says he's "waiting for the stack of hate mail. The questions above are part of a quiz which the reader can take to determine if he or she is PC. When you add your score, you can see where you fit on the scale from zero ('Get a life and please don't breed') to 250 ('Officially holier-than-thou')." Lefcowitz claims that while he "tries to represent the PC side . . . it's kind of scary." He adds that his book "has to address reality; it's not just a humor book. " Indeed, the "reality" Mr. Lefcowitz has found is apparently the same one that I have discovered, i.e., that the PC crowd will viciously attack anyone who disagrees with them, and it is, to say the least, "kind of scary" because the PC crowd are intellectual terrorists and enemies of free speech.

The *Chronicle of Higher Education* notes that "with much of the new scholarship revolving around issues of race, class, and gender, intellectual disagreements often take on a distinctly personal tone" (21 November 1990, p. A-14). Christopher Lasch, professor of history at the University of Rochester, speaks of "a climate on campuses that is tense and unforgiving . . . " and maintains that "there is a readiness to exclude other points of view because . . . they don't serve the cause of dispossessed groups" (*Chronicle*, 21 November 1990, p. A-14). Gary Marotta, Vice-President of Academic Affairs at the university where I work, said recently, "In the 1950's the right-wingers were trying to close the door to liberals. Now the other side is trying to close the door" (*The Vermilion*, 26 July 1990, p. 15).

Sterling Fishman, professor of history and education at the University of Wisconsin, concurs maintaining that, "It used to be that academic-freedom threats were from the right. But inside the university, they're now coming from the politically correct left" (*Chronicle*, 12 December 1990, p. A-16). Alan Kors, a professor of history at the University of Pennsylvania, says, "The University of Pennsylvania has become like the University of Peking," and Camille Paglia, a professor at the University of the Arts in Philadelphia, insists, "It's a fascism of the left. These people behave like the Hitler Youth" (*New York Magazine*, 21 January 1991, p. 35). Joseph S. Salemi, and adjunct associate professor of humanities at New York University, maintains that "the voice of the left-liberal orthodoxy is now the loudest, the most raucous, the best financed, and the most dangerous to academic freedom and humane discourse in the humanities." Professor Salemi goes on to point out that "this orthodoxy carries clout— in curriculum revision, in policy matters, in faculty hiring, in grants and awards, and in a thousand details of college life." He then challenges anyone who questions this to "attend a freshman orientation session, sit in a faculty dining room and listen to the conversation, encounter any of the staff from the women's studies programs or some of the younger religion or political science professors, meet any affirmative action officer, minority recruitment administrators, or diversity committees, all as ubiquitous in the academy today as commissars were under Stalin." (*Measure*, No. 102, January 1992, p. 4).

The *Chronicle of Higher Education* has also spoken of a "left-wing McCarthyism" which has led to ". . . the collapse of the liberal ideal of the university as a place of free inquiry" (*Chronicle*, 21 November 1990, p. 1). But, the cause for the greatest concern is contained in the observation of Stephan Thernstrom, a professor of history at Harvard University, who says, "This sort of atmosphere, where a few highly mobilized radical students can intimidate everyone else, is quite new. This is a new McCarthyism. It's more frightening than the old McCarthyism, which had no support in the academy. Now the enemy is within." (*New York Magazine*, 21 January 1991, p. 37).

Consider this. The American Association of University

Professors (A.A.U.P.) issued a "Statement on the Political Correctness Controversy," which claimed that "critics of political correctness had issued an attack on academe that stemmed from 'an only partly concealed animosity toward equal opportunity and its first effects of modestly increasing the participation of women and racial and cultural minorities on campus" (*Chronicle*, 4 December 1991, p. A-23). The A.A.U.P. then admitted that "more faculty members feel intimidated about speaking out on such issues as race and gender. . . ." No kidding? I wonder why. Talk about hypocrisy! In addition to the examples already cited throughout this book, consider the following specific instances of PC terrorism.

Helen Vendler, professor of English at Harvard, published "a stinging article on recent feminist literary criticism" in the May 31 issue of the *New York Review of Books*, and found herself "accused by other feminists of being cruel, cowardly, and disloyal" (*Chronicle*, 21 November 1990, p. A-15). Professor Camille Paglia of the University of the Arts in Philadelphia, who was quoted in the 15 January 1992 issue of the *Chronicle of Higher Education* as saying that she is "pleased" that more and more serious scholars are "tak[ing] shots at 'all of the wildly overinflated feminist reputations sitting like big fat ducks in academe," had an experience similar to Professor Vendler's which she discussed in an interview with *New York Magazine*.

Professor Paglia attended a presentation and lecture by a "feminist theorist from a large Ivy League university who had set out to 'decode' the subliminal sexual oppressiveness . . . [and] to expose the violent sexism . . . in fashion photography." The presentation featured slides of cosmetic ads. One was a Revlon ad of a woman standing in a pool in water up to her chin. "Decapitation!" the feminist theorist shouted. "She showed a picture of a black woman who was wearing aviator goggles and had the collar of her turtleneck sweater pulled up. 'Strangulation!' she shouted. 'Bondage!'"

When the "lecture" was over, Professor Paglia, "who considers herself a feminist, stood up and made an impassioned speech. She declared that the fashion photography of the past 40 years is great art, that instead of decapitation she saw the birth of Venus, instead of strangulation she saw references to King Tut." After Professor Paglia finished, "she was greeted, she says, 'with gasps of horror and angry murmuring. It's a form of psychosis, this slogan-filled machinery. The radical feminists have contempt for values other than their own, and they're inspiring in students a resentful attitude toward the world" (*New York Magazine*, 21 January 1991, p. 38). And it's not just the PC genderists who are doing this.

Professor Diane Ravitch of Columbia, who dared to question the validity of Afrocentrism (see chap. 3), was "derided as 'Miss Daisy' at a recent conference in Atlanta, . . . attacked in the *City Sun* and on black television and radio programs, . . ." and "has received so many threats" that she was afraid to tell an interviewer with *New York Magazine* where she lived. Professor Ravitch claims, "They've written saying things like 'We're going to get you, bitch. We're going to beat your white ass'" (*New York Magazine*, 21 January 1991, p. 40).

Michael Platt, a professor of philosophy, tells of a recent experience he had at a conference where he was called "an elitist," "a paternalist," and a "Eurocentrist." Professor Platt insisted that, "These epithets were no invitations to discussion. For one thing they neither appealed to evidence, nor offered arguments. Nor did they suggest their hurlers were ready to receive any." He went on to observe, "These denunciations were meant to knock the accused flat. 'Elitist'—socko. 'Paternalist'—take that. 'Eurocentrist'—whamo. Surrender. Come out with your hands high. This way to the sensitivity chamber!" (*Measure*, November 1991, No. 100, p. 6). As already mentioned, faculty members who opposed the politically correct writing course "Writing About Difference" (English 306) at the University of Texas at Austin maintain that they "were dismissed as right-wing fanatics, harangued by name during campus rallies, ostracized by their colleagues, and characterized as racist and sexist" (*Chronicle*, 21 November 1990, p. A-15). All these examples clearly indicate that the PC crowd uses epithets like racist, sexist, and homophobic—as well as those mentioned by Professor Platt—as carelessly as the McCarthyites of the 1950s used the word *Communist* to describe anyone who dared to dispute any of their positions.

Furthermore, as free-lance writer Lawrence Auster pointed out, "Once a scheme, no matter how inane or destructive, is defined in terms of self-evident 'fairness' and 'truth,' how can any decent person think critically about it, much less oppose it?" (*Measure*, November 1991, No. 100, p. 4). In other words, even the name of the movement, political *correctness* presupposes that anyone who disputes its positions is *in*correct. It's simple. If I am PC, and you disagree with me, you're incorrect. And by the way, you're an elitist, racist, sexist, paternalistic, Eurocentric homophobe, too—end of discussion; turn out the lights; the party's over. See how easy?

The PC crowd now maintains that the name, political correctness, began as a kind of self-deprecating joke and has now adopted different names for the movement (like multiculturalism and gender feminism). But even though the names are changed, the contradictions, the hypocrisy, the complete intolerance of other positions, and the penchant for using *ad hominem* logic to end discussion remains in all the PC "isms."And students are getting into the act also.

According to *New York Magazine*, there was a course taught at Harvard University called "Peopling of America." The course was team-taught by Stephan Thernstrom, editor of the *Harvard Encyclopedia of American Ethnic Groups*, and Bernard Bailyn, winner of two Pulitzer Prizes. Even though the course had been offered for some time without incident, articles suddenly began appearing in the *Harvard Crimson*, the school newspaper, accusing both professors, who, incidentally, "have solid liberal democratic credentials," of "racial insensitivity." Initially, the charges were anonymous, but the students responsible for the articles finally came forward with a list of grievances. Professor Bailyn had read from the diary of a southern planter, but not from that of a slave, which, the students maintained, "was a covert defense of slavery." When Bailyn pointed out that he was not aware of any journals, diaries, or letters written by slaves, the students said that, under those circumstances, he should not have read from the plantation owner's diary, either.

Professor Thernstrom demonstrated his "racial insensitivity" by using the word "Indian" instead of "native American." He also used the term "Oriental," which, the students claimed, was racist. He also assigned a book which mentioned that affirmative action is considered by some to be discriminatory. But most egregiously, Professor Thernstrom endorsed in class Senator Patrick Moynihan's PNC idea that the major cause of black poverty is the disintegration of the black family. "It's like being called a Commie in the fifties," Thernstrom says. "Whatever explanation you offer, once accused, you're always suspect" (*New York Magazine*, 21 January 1991, p. 34). Although both Bailyn and Thernstrom initially defended themselves against the charges, they finally decided it was more trouble than it was worth, and their course, "Peopling of America," is no longer offered at Harvard.

A similar episode occurred at San Francisco State University. Robert C. Smith, a newly recruited black professor of political science, offered a new course in black politics. Now it would seem that this course would be very PC, right? Wrong! Oba T'Shaka, chairman of Black Studies at San Francisco State, maintained that Smith's course "was a veiled attempt to put us [the Black Studies Department] out of business, . . . to farm out black studies to European departments under the name of multi-culturalism." According to the *Chronicle of Higher Education*, student activists and professors not only complained, they conspired to sabotage Professor Smith's class. "Mr. Smith's course was disrupted for several days, then all the black students dropped it, leaving only five white students." Professor Smith maintains that the disruption of his class "was an attempt to impose by intimidation a particular view of how the curriculum should be organized" (*Chronicle*, 1 May 1991, p. A-11). Sorry, Mr. Smith. You're PNC, so you have no right to complain.

Linda Chavez is a Mexican-American woman, a former director of the U. S. Commission on Civil Rights, a senior Fellow at the Manhattan Institute for Policy and Research, and author of the book, *Out of the Barrio: Toward a New Politics of Hispanic Assimilation*, published in October of 1991 by Basic Books. Sounds pretty PC to me. According to the *Chronicle of Higher Education*, Ms. Chavez was asked to deliver the commencement address at the University of Northern Colorado in 1990, but her appearance was cancelled "after some minority students objected." Confused? Just wait. Ms. Chavez was asked by a member of the student-government association at Arizona State University to speak to Hispanic students, but was then extended an invitation to speak as part of a broader lecture series on campus. She then received a letter from Deborah Kaye, a junior at Arizona State and director of the lecture series, informing her that her appearance had been cancelled because of "student opposition." It was also reported that this "student opposition" had been initiated by "an Hispanic student group!" Huh? Well, maybe this will help clear up the mystery.

Linda Chavez, you see, served under President Reagan and has been an outspoken critic of affirmative action and "bilingual" education (see chap. 2). The letter she received from Arizona State informing her that her speaking engagement had been cancelled also said, "The Minority

Coalition [a minority student organization at Arizona State] has requested that we cancel this engagement and bring other speakers whose views are more in line with their politics" (*Chronicle*, 11 September 1991, p. A-19). While the kind of honesty contained in this letter is refreshing, the admission is horrifying, but it comes as no surprise. "Ms. Chavez called the incident at Arizona State 'an example, not just of political correctness, but of a double standard being applied to blacks and Hispanics who hold conservative opinions. We are not allowed to deviate from the orthodoxy of the civil-rights establishment" (*Chronicle*, 11 September 1991, p. A-20).

Here's another good one. Thomas Lauer was scheduled to serve as a visiting assistant professor at Seattle University, but his appointment was cancelled because, "according to a university statement, officials feared the campus opposition to the appointment could disrupt 'the university's ordinary educational processes'" (*Chronicle*, 2 October 1991, p. A-4). It turns out that Mr. Lauer was an officer of the Central Intelligence Agency (C.I.A.), and that was the reason for the "officials' fears." Now, am I to understand that there are actually people on college campuses today who would not only pass up the chance to find out what they could from a C.I.A. officer, but would also deny that opportunity to other students who might be interested in taking advantage of such a learning experience? Is *this* what academe has turned into? Here's the real kicker. According to the *Chronicle of Higher Education*, Mr. Lauer's services were being provided *at no cost* to the university because the C.I.A. was giving him a sabbatical leave to take the appointment, and the agency had agreed to pay his salary!

So intense are the intimidation efforts of the PC crowd on campuses all across the country that James David Barber, professor of political science and policy studies at Duke University, has questioned whether it is even possible any longer "to discuss black or women's studies in a reasonable way without being called racist or sexist" (*Chronicle*, 21 November 1991, p. A-14). For instance, is it even possible today for one to suggest that it is, to say the least, curious that the birthday of Martin Luther King is a national holiday and the birthdays of George Washington and Abraham Lincoln are not without being called a racist? Talk about living on the edge.

While working on this manuscript, I read papers which were excerpts from this book at academic conferences on four separate occasions. I have been attacked each time and called "paranoid" and "simple minded" (in addition to all the other PC epithets), and I have been accused of oversimplifying the issue, quoting out of context, and misquoting altogether. These attacks have been as brutal as they have been consistent. My position is that those academicians who hold PNC views have simply chosen to remain silent rather than subject themselves to the kind of treatment to which I have become so accustomed.

The observation that members at the professoriate who hold views that are more conservative than the academic mainstream have chosen silence over confrontation led Professor Catharine Stimpson of Rutgers University to ask on a nationally televised panel on PC which aired on public television, "Whence courage?" One of my colleagues said the same thing to me when I said that a deafening silence had settled over academe because of all the intimidation. "So you people don't have the courage of your convictions?" he asked. My response was that no one likes being called hateful names nor do our conservative colleagues in the professoriate feel the need to place themselves in a position where they have to justify their existence to Catharine Stimpson or any other abusive PC individual. But there is much, much more to this PC intimidation than merely the fear of being called ugly names.

In an interview with me (see chap. 7), Dr. Burton Raffel, Eminent Scholar of Humanities at my university, said, "I have had former graduates of mine tell me, and

this is incredible to me, that in job interviews the chairmen
of departments where they're trying to get a job have asked
them to identify themselves ideologically to see whether
they fit with the ideology of the department. Now this has
no place. . . . or the business of Stanley Fish, who ought
to be absolutely ashamed of himself."

Stanley Fish, head of the Department of English at
Duke University, provides a clear and indisputable example of PC intimidation. He was quoted as saying that
people "with illiberal attitudes toward new scholarship
should not be appointed to sit on committees which deal
with promotion and tenure matters" (*Chronicle*, 21 November 1990, p. A-14). I'm sure the conservatives in Mr.
Fish's department are clamoring to get their views heard.
Professor Raffel said, "This [is] Hitlerism in the name of
PCism."

There is also concern among faculty that PC thinking
has come to affect hiring and promotion practices. Professor Stimpson, the one who questioned the "courage"
of the PNC professoriate, also said, "The attack on diversity [aka, political correctness and its "isms"] is a rhetorical
strategy by neo-conservatives who have their own political
agenda. Under the guise of defending objectivity and intellectual rigor, which is a lot of mishmash, they are trying
to preserve the cultural and political supremacy of white
heterosexual males" (*New York Magazine*, 21 January
1991, p. 35). Now Catharine Stimpson just happens to be
the dean of the graduate school at Rutgers, a curious
testament to what she calls "the supremacy of white
heterosexual males." But in addition to the obvious contradiction, her position gives her the authority to use her
administrative muscle to penalize any ordinary faculty
member who would dare to take issue with her very PC
statements. I would ask Dean Stimpson if she would care
to argue for the position that there is no such thing as
academic politics and that faculty members' careers are
not affected by such things? Not only would no sane

academic argue such a position, I assert that Henry Kissinger
was right when he said, "Academic politics are the most
vicious of all because the stakes are so small." In other
words, how dare Dean Stimpson ask so smugly from high
atop her administrative pulpit, "Whence courage?" My
response would be, "Whence fairness?" Professor Joseph
Salemi of N.Y.U. contends that people who dare question
[this] hegemony, which has become institutionalized in the
education establishment, have their careers ruined or cut
short" (*Measure*, No. 102, January 1992, p. 4).

Perhaps even more intimidating, questions of political
correctness have found their way into accrediting practices.
Raymond F. Bacchetti is acting vice-president for planning
and management at Standford University and chair of the
Accrediting Commission for Senior Colleges and Universities of the Western Association of Schools and Colleges.
Stephen S. Weiner is executive director of the commission.
These two men co-authored a piece which was published
in the 8 May 1991 issue of the *Chronicle of Higher Education*
the title of which was "Diversity Is a Key Factor in Educational Quality and Hence in Accreditation." Here are
some excerpts from that article:

> Racial and ethnic diversity raises a set of issues
> that are central to educational content and quality,
> and therefore, to the work of accreditation. . . .
> Wide agreement exists among institutions in our
> region that diversity is an important element in the
> content and purpose of higher education and, there-
> fore, is an appropriate part of the agenda of our
> commission. . . .
> We urge campuses to use the accreditation
> process, and particularly the institutional self-
> studyit includes, to address diversity issues. . . .

To understand the significance of such statements, one
must understand that if a university or college loses its
accreditation, it loses funding, and, of course, students. In
other words, losing accreditation would be the kiss of death

for an institution of higher learning. When those responsible for deciding whether or not an institution should be
accredited call for "educational content" which "address[es]
diversity issues," administrations, departments, and faculty
simply have no choice but to adjust to meet those demands
or risk losing accreditation.

The Baton Rouge *Sunday Advocate* ran an Associated
Press story on 20 October 1991, which recounted an episode that occurred at prestigious Wellesley College.
According to that story, the administration of the all-girl
school hired a lesbian, Michele Porche, and her live-in
partner, a twenty-eight-year-old graduate student named
Stacy Homan, to run a dormitory. Jill Keegan, student
president of Lake House, one of the dorms on the campus
of Wellesley, said, "The fact that Michele was hired and
was put in a setting where she is working directly with
students is a strong indication of Wellesley's commitment
to multiculturalism." While some protested the hiring of
a lesbian to run an all-girl's dorm and questioned the board
of trustees' inclusion of homosexuality under the rubric
of multiculturalism, that was easily dismissed as PNC.
"More startling," Associated Press writer Ceci Connolly
said, "was the outcry from the *other* side of the spectrum."

It seems that Ms. Porche was hired to run Dower
Dormitory. At the last minute, she was assigned to Lake
House Dormitory. Now, because Lake House has no first-
year students, the move was interpreted as an attempt to
"hide" Porche and her partner from the younger students.
It was called "a cop out," and many demanded to know
why the school would "bother hiring an openly lesbian
couple if you hide them from the younger women?"
Dorothee Harmon, a student at Wellesley and a member
of Wellesley Lesbians, Bisexuals and Friends, said, "We
felt it was a betrayal, because it was an acknowledgment
that homophobia was okay. Not only was Michele discriminated against, but the whole campus was, in the notion that
everybody had to participate in this protection from
homophobia." Now, I ask you, is this looking for something

to argue about or what? But, as Ceci Connolly points out, "Sometimes even politically correct isn't enough." But it certainly helps if you want to run a dorm at Wellesley.

While being PC clearly seems to put one on the "academic fast track," the reverse also holds; being PNC puts one on a lonely road to nowhere. Norman S. Holland, assistant professor of Hispano Literatures at Hampshire College, maintains that "he was denied reappointment because several of his colleagues accused him of being 'Eurocentric' in his approach to the field and questioned his commitment to the college's Third World Studies program." Professor Holland stated, "I don't want to believe in a tyranny of the left, but that is what's happened to me" (*Chronicle*, 21 November 1990, p. A-14).

Yet another example of professors being penalized professionally for being politically incorrect involves Steven Mosher, who was a professor at Stanford and under that university's employ when he went to China in the early 1980s to investigate "China's policy of forced abortions." According to the *Chronicle of Higher Education*, although "few if any scholars questioned the accuracy of Mr. Mosher's work," there arose a "controversy over his behavior in China." Apparently, Mosher contradicted the official party line on the issue of forced abortions, which is a sensitive and difficult one for the PC crowd. Professor Mosher maintained, "It wasn't through the efforts of China watchers that we saw China for what it was." Obviously, if one follows the PC position of abortion to its logical conclusion, the concepts of forced and selective abortions are quite reasonable. For instance, in some countries, people have economic incentives to intentionally abort only female babies. Well, why not? We're not dealing with a human being, right? And it's simply the woman's choice, right? Nevertheless, Professor Mosher "was dismissed in 1983 from Stanford's graduate program in anthropology" (*Chronicle*, 30 January 1991, p. A-16). He is now director of the Asian Studies Center at the Claremont Institute.

In 1987, the University of Alabama, in response

to student complaints, disciplined Phillip A. Bishop, associate professor and director of the university's Human Performance Laboratory. The university demanded that Professor Bishop "stop injecting religious beliefs into classes" and warned him "to stop holding optional classes in which he taught from a 'Christian perspective'" (*Chronicle*, 17 April 1991, p. A-1). Professor Bishop sued the university in 1988 maintaining that his right of free speech had been violated. The court ruled in Bishop's favor in 1990, but the 11th Circuit Court of Appeals recently rendered a decision reversing the lower court's decision and upholding the university's right to so discipline a faculty member. Even the A.A.U.P. and the A.C.L.U. have expressed serious concern over this decision.

To really top it off, according to the *Chronicle of Higher Education*, students at the University of Vermont took over the president's office several times during 1991 "claiming the university had not followed policies designed to attract and retain minority students." Apparently the protests were so intense that the president of the university, George H. Davis, *resigned*, saying, "It is apparent that support for my leadership is not sufficiently strong for me to carry on what I started" (*Chronicle*, 30 October 1991, p. A-4). How about that? The PC crowd went and bagged 'em a university president!

On the same page of the story of Mr. Davis is the story of yet another university president who resigned. John T. Wolfe, Jr., the president of Kentucky State University, resigned just as the Board of Regents began an investigation into "nine charges against him, including one allegation that he had unilaterally raised his own salary from $92,000 a year to almost $101,000." Approximately seventy-five students took over the administration building for two days to demonstrate their support for Mr. Wolfe and to urge the board "to retain Kentucky State's mission as a historically black institution" (*Chronicle*, 30 October 1991, p. A-4). While the former president was not reinstated, all charges against him were dropped; and he was retained "through July of 1992 as a consultant" for which he will receive $69,374.97. Notice a difference between the treatment received by Mr. Wolfe and Mr. Davis? Oh, did I forget to mention that Mr. Wolfe is black?

The concern over this kind of pressure to conform to PC thinking and agendas has become so pronounced and widespread that an organization called The National Association of Scholars (N.A.S.) was formed. Based at Princeton University in New Jersey, the association "offers a forum to professors who have felt inhibited from questioning affirmative-action programs, required courses on ethnic diversity, and other issues" (*Chronicle*, 12 December 1990, p. A-1). Stanley Fish, chairman of the Department of English at Duke, responded to the formation of the association by writing a letter to the campus newspaper in which he, predictably, called the N.A.S. "racist, sexist, and homophobic." Professor Burton Raffel responded to this by saying, "This is not only slanderous, it's also a lie. I'm a member of the organization, and I am none of those things" (see chap. 7). I concur with Dr. Raffel and find Mr. Fish's comments unconscionable and the antithesis of what a university is supposed to be.

It is not just faculty members, however, who have been subjected to intimidation of this kind. Students have also been subjected to PC intellectual terrorism. According to *Citizen* magazine, a young woman from Georgia, Jane Bailey, enrolled in a master's program at Rutgers University. A term paper she submitted "on the theme of oath-taking in Shakespeare's *The Merchant of Venice*" was returned with the criticism that it was "too moral." On another occasion, a student was told by the instructor not to refer "to the morality of a literary work. 'I prefer to use the word *politics*,' Bailey recalls the instructor saying. 'I felt silenced in that class,' Bailey said. 'There was a reluctance to discuss traditional values'" (*Citizen*, 21 October 1991, p. 14).

Remember the feminist instructor at the University of Washington at Seattle who asserted in class that "the traditional American family represents a dysfunctional family unit?" Remember? "Students who questioned this assertion were shouted down by teaching assistants yelling 'denial, denial' in unison," and when a male student asked the instructor *after class* about the evidence on which her assertions rested, he found himself "barred from attending the class by the campus police" (*Citizen*, 21 October 1991, p. 15).

According to the *Chronicle of Higher Education*, at the University of Maryland, students who flew American flags out of their dorm windows during Desert Storm were encouraged to take them down. Even though the university finally relented and allowed students to display their flags, these students were criticized by some of the same individuals who had not long before applauded the Supreme Court decision on flag burning.

An episode at the University of Hawaii contains a compelling irony which is yet another example of PC hypocrisy. According to the *Chronicle of Higher Education*, Joey Carter, a student at the university in Manoa, wrote a column in the campus paper "about the difficulties of being a white male in Hawaii" and claimed he had been the victim of "Caucasian-bashing." Haunani-Kay Trask, a professor and director of the Center for Hawaiian Studies, responded to Mr. Carter's column in a column of her own in which she informed Carter that his presence in Hawaii was a "luxury provided him by centuries of white conquest" and that "Hawaiians could certainly benefit from one less 'haole' [white person] in our land." She also informed Mr. Carter that "United Airlines has dozens of flights to the U. S. continent everyday." Professor Trask concluded by saying, "Mr. Carter, why don't you take one?" (*Chronicle*, 5 December 1990, p. A-2).

At Brown University, Douglas Hann, a junior, was expelled for shouting anti-black and anti-homosexual remarks, "at no one in particular," while celebrating his twenty-first birthday. According to the *Chronicle of Higher*

Education, it was ruled by a university discipline committee that Mr. Hann "violated the university's policy that prohibits the 'subjection of another person, group, or class of persons to inappropriate, abusive, threatening, or demeaning actions, based on race, religion, gender, handicap, ethnicity, national origin, or sexual orientation'" (*Chronicle*, 20 February 1991, p. A-2). Again, the A.C.L.U. has expressed concern over this episode, and a similar anti-harassment policy at the University of Wisconsin is now being challenged in court. Still, "a recent study by the Carnegie Foundation for the Advancement of Teaching found that 70 percent of the nation's colleges have enacted or are considering enacting speech codes" (*Citizen*, 21 October 1991, p. 14).

But let us assume one sincerely does not want to offend a person of African descent. What does one call that person? Negro? Black? Afro-American? Afri-American? African-American? I have heard black people refer to themselves by all these names. I have even heard a black man on the news one morning, an air force pilot, say that he wants to be referred to as a Black American and that he is offended by any other name. So what *does* one do? What does one say? How does one avoid offending? What if one does not wish to offend a homosexual person. What does one call that individual? Homosexual? Gay? Lesbian? Is a lesbian a homosexual, or is that something different? Professor Eve Sedgwick, who has been called by one of her own colleagues "part mascot, part earth mother to the gay and lesbian studies movement," says, "I prefer the term queer" (*Chronicle*, 24 October 1990, p. A-6). So, again, what does one do? What does one say? Is this ridiculous or what?

It seems clear that because of their hyperbolic sensitivity, there is simply no way to avoid offending PC persons. It seems equally clear that these people are bound and determined to be offended regardless of how others talk about them.

The terrorist tactics of the PC crowd reveals the true nature of the entire movement. Its assertions rest on shoddy, unprofessional, or non-existent scholarship; its logic is either *ad hominem* or contradictory, and its condemnations are clear examples of gross, naked hypocrisy. But, as I have already pointed out, not everyone in the professoriate today is PC, and politically correct terrorist tactics and deconstructive games notwithstanding, more and more faculty members and administrators are speaking out all across the country. It is in their protests that we can discover, at least in part, the road back to sanity.

Chapter 6

THE ROAD BACK TO SANITY

If I might offer an analogy, consider that the road to excellence in education is a brand new interstate, sleek and straight. That being the case, the path that we, in this country, are on is a bumpy, dusty, curvy, back-country lane. Admittedly, some of the scenery is interesting, but we are not making very good time en route to our destination. And, while we are puttering along sight-seeing on our country road, the rest of the nations of the world are on that interstate "with the hammer down." So what do we do? How do we get off "the collision course with the reality that America is producing a second-class work force?" Even though we can anticipate that the PC crowd in the educational establishment will object to every turn we take in order to make our way back to that interstate to excellence, we simply must begin to find our way toward the road back to sanity.

As mentioned in chapter 2, one thing that needs to be done is a major restructuring of the welfare system, which, again, can only be described as an economic disaster and a moral disgrace that has victimized the very people it was designed to help. It goes without saying that all decent people recognize that they have a moral obligation to provide for those who are incapable of taking care of themselves. Having said that, it is equally important that intelligent people realize that it is possible to help people *too* much, thus turning individuals who would otherwise be perfectly capable of fending for themselves into dependent victims of our misplaced compassion.

Dr. Ben Carson, director of pediatric neurosurgery at Johns Hopkins University, who happens to be black and who was mentioned in chapter 3, compared the effects of the welfare system to what he called "The Grizzly Bear Syndrome." He told the story of the grizzly bears at a national park which were perfectly self-sufficient until tourists started feeding them. At that point, the bears got lazy and forgot how to hunt. Dr. Carson also pointed out that although this was not the bears' fault; they were the victims.

I believe that Dr. Carson's story is perfectly analogous, and we must revise welfare programs so that they empower rather than enable. We need programs that will reinvigorate the traditional family unit in the minority community because there is simply no way that government will ever be able to provide the support that a family structure can. I am convinced that restructuring welfare programs so that benefits are tied to socially responsible behavior would do more than anything else we can do to solve the discipline problems in our schools. But we must move forward with compassion for those who, like the grizzly bears in Dr. Carson's story, have been victimized by the system, and we must be patient because it will take time for the positive effects of such reforms to be felt. It could take a whole generation or even more, but let us begin.

We must also seek to change the "victim mentality" which has taken hold in this country. I place the blame for this mentality, which is deeply rooted in American culture today, right at the doorstep of the PC crowd for, as Professor Diane Ravitch points out, they are "promoting a brand of history in which everyone is either a descendant of victims or oppressors" (*New York Magazine*, 21 January 1991, p. 40). This victim mentality is very convenient as it allows people to blame all their failures on others. Interestingly enough, in the Greek epic *The Odyssey*, Zeus addresses this very point. In the very beginning, Zeus says, "What a lamentable thing it is that men should blame the gods and regard us as the source of their troubles when it is their own wickedness which brings them sufferings worse than any which Destiny allots them" (Rieu Translation, p. 26). The point, of course, is that this tendency to look for scapegoats and to blame others for all the bad things that happen in our lives was not invented by the PC crowd. It is as old as mankind (or should I say *person*kind) itself and runs very deep in the human (or, if you prefer, humyn) psyche. It is always easier to make excuses and to blame others than to pick yourself up, dust yourself off, and get back in the race. The "Poor me; I'm a victim" syndrome was even demonstrated by the chief executives of America's three largest automobile manufacturers when, on President Bush's recent trip to Japan, they spent the entire time whining to the international media about how unfair the Japanese were. That was most embarrassing, and the Japanese were correct in raising the question of just why these and other American corporate executives have salaries and perks which are not tied to their companies' performance.

This is *not* to say that discrimination never existed. To be sure, it did, but, as stated in chapter 3, we set about trying to rectify that almost thirty years ago, and, as Professor Dennis of Columbia points out, "the letter of the law . . . long ago outdistanced the spirit of the law" in these matters. In other words, we are now in the punitive stage where we are trying to compensate for historical inequities, as though that were even possible to do. In fact, it would not be altogether invalid to state that white, heterosexual males of European descent are now the group most discriminated against in the United States. There are no special programs for us, no set asides, no quotas. And, you know what? *I don't want any!* Level the playing field; make the rules consistent, and I'll compete, and if I'm not good at one thing, then I'll try something else. But, for crying out loud, it's time for this nation to get up off its "pity-pot" and back into the international economy.

Unfortunately, reorganizing our thinking to purge the "victim mentality" which has taken hold will also take time. There are, however, other specific things that can and must be done now which will have more immediate effects in improving educational quality in this country. Reforms instituted in the state of Tennessee provide a number of examples of things which have worked, and those reforms can serve as signposts pointing out clear paths for us to follow.

In 1979, Tennessee was regarded as backward. Its people were uneducated; its political system hopelessly corrupt, and its governor was about to be convicted and sent to prison. The state was losing two hundred thousand jobs per year and picking up about twenty thousand. Amid this darkness, the people of Tennessee turned to a young reform candidate for governor who made an absolute commitment to improving Tennessee's educational system, even if it meant letting the highways crumble. After this man became governor and instituted some basic reforms in the educational system, new capital investment in Tennessee tripled. When a major automobile manufacturer (Saturn) decided to locate its new facility outside of Nashville, the president of that manufacturer, Bill Hoglund, told reporters that they chose Tennessee because "we liked Tennessee's commitment to excellence in education. Especially the idea of paying teachers more for performance because that's what we're going to have to do if we are going to compete with the Japanese." By the way, as an added bonus, after the new governor reformed that state's educational system, nearly 10 percent of all Japanese investment in the United States now goes to Tennessee. All because a governor made a no-nonsense, no-excuses commitment to reform and improve the state's educational system. That man was Lamar Alexander.

I had the pleasure of meeting and speaking to Mr. Alexander at a fund-raising luncheon for a friend of mine who was running for governor of Louisiana. No, it wasn't David Duke or Edwin Edwards. It was Congressman Bob Livingston, and it was in Baton Rouge in 1987. Anyway,

Mr. Alexander had already completed his second term as governor of Tennessee and had just returned from an extended trip to Australia. He was most gracious and forthcoming, even to the point of sending me a copy of his farewell address as governor.

In that address, Mr. Alexander said that when he undertook to overhaul the educational system of Tennessee, "the hardest problem was trying to apply common sense to the deep ruts into which public education had fallen." His common sense told him that eighth graders should know eighth grade skills, that citizens and not politicians should set the standards for their schools, that parents should be given a choice as to which schools their children would attend, that graduates with liberal arts degrees should be allowed to teach, and that better teachers should be paid more. His ideas were called "unfair," "impractical," "outrageous," and "elitist." *Elitist!* Whoa, that's a PC term, and we're talking 1979. Still, Lamar Alexander pushed forward with his reforms with incredible results. Mr. Alexander is now the Secretary of Education for the Bush administration. It seems to me that good common sense is sorely lacking in much of the PC movement. Let us hope that Secretary Alexander can, with similar results, "apply common sense to some of the deep ruts into which public education [has] fallen" all across this country, but he needs help. He needs help from the producers and consumers of education. The professionals in education who are paid to teach are the producers, and parents who pay the taxes which pay the teachers and students who are the products and/or victims of the process of public education in the United States are the consumers. Even working adults with no children have a stake in this because they still pay taxes which fund the process and they will either have to hire and/or work with the products of that process. So, we *all* have a share in the responsibility, and each of us has a role to play.

We, the professionals in the education establishment,

bear the bulk of the responsibility simply because we are paid to. Therefore, we must answer for what has happened. Some of us are guilty by our silence. We have allowed outlandish theories based on shoddy scholarship to go unchallenged, and some of our PC colleagues have pushed these theories onto their students as fact. This has started to change as more and more of our PNC colleagues have begun to speak out. Some of those courageous enough to challenge the PC crowd have been mentioned throughout this book. Highly respected scholars in all fields such as Arthur Schlesinger, Henry Louis Gates, Gertrude Himmelfarb, Cornel West, John Silber, Everette E. Dennis, Maxine Hairston, Gary Marotta, Diane Ravitch, Christian Sommers, Burton Raffell, and Lynne Cheney have come forward and spoken out against some of the nonsense spawned by political correctness and all its attendant "isms," and those challenges have not been to the PC crowd's morality or their patriotism, but, appropriately, to their professionalism, or the lack of it, both in their teaching and in their scholarship.

For instance, when the PC crowd at the University of Texas at Austin began pushing their course "Writing About Difference" (English 306), with its "strongly political message" and its "proposed readings" which some faculty considered to be "consistently leftist," many faculty members spoke out. Alan Gribben, a professor of English at U.T. and the chief critic of English 306 claimed, "They've turned the course upside down. Where we used to have chapters devoted to grammar, we now have chapters devoted to oppression" (Chronicle, 21 November 1990, p. A-15). Maxine Hairston, a professor of English at U.T., past chairman of the Conference on College Composition and Communication (the four C's), and a person who describes herself as a "solid liberal," says "she views the course [English 306] as an attempt to promote politically correct ideas" (Chronicle, 21 November 1990, p. A-15). Most importantly, Professor Hairston also maintains that "the proposed course is pedagogically unsound, a retreat from everything we've learned about teaching writing in the past 15 years" (*Chronicle*, 23 January 1991, p. B-1). This is what ultimately makes something unacceptable from a scholarly point of view. In other words, what is it that we're supposed to be doing in college composition classes—indoctrinating students to particular points of view or teaching them how to write in such a way that will give them a competitive edge? And what about in our literature classes?

What finally attracted me to the study of literature as a career was when I developed an appreciation of what makes literary art "great." What makes one work "great" and another mediocre is that the "great" one will, in some way, have the inherent ability to transcend time and space so that it can speak to all peoples in all times. Herein lies the "greatness" of a truly fine work of literary art, or, for that matter, any other kind of art.

Joel Oppenheimer, a poet and playwright from New York and the subject of my dissertation, put it very succinctly. In an interview with me, he described the movement of "great" art as going "so deeply into the personal that you come out the other side and it becomes the general. At that point, the experience has validity and meaning for others." In other words, the reader of a "great" book does *not* respond by thinking, "Wow, this writer is a genius." A reader's response to a truly "great" book would be, according to Oppenheimer, "Oh yeah, I've been there, too." Actually, Joel was simply paraphrasing Alexander Pope who defined "great" poetry as "What oft was thought, but ne'er so well expressed."

Great literature, in other words, is not limited by race or gender or anything else. It bypasses all such ephemeral considerations and drives to the very core of human existence and the human condition. It allows us, as Edgar Allan Poe put it, to "soar with an undaunted wing. . . . To seek for treasure in the jewelled skies." It also allows

us to peek into eternity, glimpse the face of God, and see
the world, as Sir Philip Sydney put it, "not as it is, but
as it could be and as it should be." Or to use Bobby
Kennedy's paraphrase of Sydney, "Some men see things
as they are and say why; I see things that never were and
say why not?"

The entire politically correct movement runs exactly
counter to this, pushing ethnic fundamentalism which, as
Professor Henry Gates pointed out, is itself racist and
which presupposes, as Professor Diane Ravitch pointed
out, "that children can learn only from the experiences of
people from the same race." Consider, for instance, the
complaint raised in my class one day by one of my students
about a T-shirt she had seen (which one can see on virtually
any campus today) worn by a black student which said,
"It's a black thing; you wouldn't understand." All during
the Clarence Thomas/Anita Hill soap opera, I heard over
and over again women on the news and in person say things
like, "Men just don't get it." In other words, all the PC
"isms" have, to borrow from Joel Oppenheimer, gone so
deeply into the personal that they are stuck and cannot
or do not want to come out the other side to where the
experience will have validity and meaning for others. This
kind of treehouse mentality is not only anti-intellectual,
it is rather juvenile, and the PC crowd must be forced by
bonafide scholars to address these fundamental questions
and issues in virtually every field and discipline.

In the field of history, Lynne V. Chenney, chairman
of the NEH, rejects the PC position and maintains, "We
shouldn't think of history as simply a political tool"
(*Newsweek*, 23 September 1991, p. 46). Kenneth Jackson
of Columbia University said in an interview on ABC's
"Nightline," "The students, soon enough, will begin to
resent that and come to believe that history is a kind of
political document, and they'll have no more use for it
in the United States than they've had for a generation in
Eastern Europe where they believe that history is some

sort of propaganda with no basis in reality." These and all the other prominent historians already mentioned agree that when history *is* used as a political tool, it ceases to be history at all. Former Secretary of Education William Bennett, who appeared on the same program with Professor Jackson, agreed and said, "If history is not the disinterested pursuit of the truth, then to heck with it. If it's just determined by what the power relations are, then just take the whole darn thing out because it's just another cynical exercise in power politics." Mr. Bennett's statement could easily be expanded to include not just history, but all intellectual disciplines.

Professor Jackson goes on to make the incredibly significant point that, "It is precisely because we do not have in the United States a common ethnicity or a common race or a common religion that history, American history, is so important. That is all we *do* have as a people to hold us together." Even Governor Mario Cuomo of New York is reported by ABC's "Nightline" to have said that this refocusing of history " . . . tears at the consensus of cultures that is the essence of America." William Bennett also stated on that program, "You cannot deny the significant fact of Western civilization and its *dominant* influence on the shape of America." I agree, and I also maintain that any "history" that, in fact, ignores or downplays that influence is a lie, political propaganda at its worst. Mr. Bennett went on to say, "The books the founders wrote, read, and the influence of the West in our traditions is nothing to be embarrassed about."

Michael Platt, professor of political philosophy, concurs and asks some crucial questions which demand answers if honesty has not become yet another victim of PC. "What if," Professor Platt demands to know, "it is simply true that in the geography of human achievement some regions and times have contributed more than others? And what if it is simply true, when all is said by way of qualification, that Europe has contributed more? And even that it has contributed the most, and might, therefore, be called central, and even preeminent?" (*Measure*, Nov. 1991, No. 100, p. 7). Professor Platt also maintains that, in terms of relative contributions to civilization, "Europe is central because central to its contributions, in truth its greatest contribution, is the discovery that something above Europe or any region or culture is more important to man as man . . . not man as creature of culture or convention or geography" (*Measure*, p. 7). In this observation, Professor Platt has likened history to "great" art.

Professor Diane Ravitch of Columbia agrees and warns, "We're also in danger of forgetting that the Western tradition has been the great liberating tradition in history, the source of ideals and individual freedom and political democracy to which most of the world now aspires" (*Chronicle*, 30 January 1991, p. A-15). Professor Ravitch points out in an article she wrote which was published in the 24 October 1991 issue of the *Chronicle of Higher Education* that there is a significant difference between a "pluralistic approach" to education and a "particularist" approach. "The particularist approach to American culture can be seen most vividly in ethnic-studies programs whose goal is to 'raise self-esteem' of [particular] students." The pluralist approach, on the other hand, "recognizes that the common culture has been shaped by the interaction of the nation's many diverse cultural elements." But this whole concept of "pluralism" is not only not new, it too has inherent problems.

As already mentioned in chapter 3, in 1977, Gary Marotta, Vice President of Academic Affairs at my university, wrote an article entitled "Cultural Pluralism: Promises and Problems," which was published in *Perspectives on Bilingual-Bicultural Education*. In the footnotes to his article, Professor Marotta cites Richard Pratte's "The Concept of Cultural Pluralism," which was published in *Proceedings of the Philosophy of Education Society* in 1972 to define "cultural pluralism." Consider the definition. "Cultural pluralism obtains where diverse groups of commensurate legal status coexist within a society, while retaining distinct identities and cultures." I submit that politically correct multiculturalism has become an alias for what was called "cultural pluralism" in the 1970s. In fact, Professor Marotta even uses the word "multicultural" in the article. In other words, the comments about cultural pluralism contained in this 1977 article would also apply to what is now called PC multiculturalism, and those comments are, perhaps, even more relevant and salient today.

Professor Marotta maintains, cultural pluralism was "born of rage and protest." He goes on to say that "it has superseded the contesting models of 'assimilation' and 'melting pot'" (p. 29). He further states, "It has been argued that pluralism acquiesces to the *status quo* and that it relies on a relativism which retrogresses into group chauvinism. To paraphrase Karl Popper, the closed, tribal or organic community is both fundamentally anti-individualistic and anti-humanitarian" (p. 30). Professor Marotta also points out that the "misconceptions" spawned by pluralism "are distorting educational policy" and concludes that "pluralism must go beyond polemics to prove itself consistent with American theories of democracy and merit" (p. 31). He also quotes Bayard Rustin, then President of the Philip Randolph Institute, who calls pluralism a "hoax and a trap" and "an obstacle to a broad-based struggle for social justice." Then Professor Marotta asks the most important questions of all: "Does pluralism's invitation to difference perpetuate suspicion and resentment? Does it encourage the very prejudice it seeks to eliminate? . . . Will pluralism exacerbate differences, leading to the bankruptcy of shared values and the dissolution of civic and national bonds? Will America, if it does not dissolve into its plural components, remain at best fragmented or Balkanized?" (pp. 30-31).

In essence, I think that Professors Ravitch and Marotta

are in agreement in that they recognize that there is an
American culture that is completely and totally different
from any other in the world, and a black-American female
living in New York today actually has more in common
culturally with *me*, a white American male, than she does
with a black female living in Africa. Likewise, simply
because I am a "Cajun" by heritage does *not* mean that
I have more in common with my French ancestors than
I do with my American contemporaries. So while all of
us can and should be aware of and even celebrate our varied
ancestral heritages (An', lemme tell you, *cher*, Cajuns
really know how to do dat!), we must always remember
that it is this very diversity which makes *American* culture
so rich and unique. I, for one, am not only proud, I am
grateful to be a part of *that* cultural experience.

I think that both Professor Ravitch and Professor
Marotta are saying that the PC multiculturalists, whether
we call them pluralists or particularists, either forgot this,
never understood it in the first place, or simply refuse to
admit it, and there is a real danger in this. Professor Ravitch
even goes so far as to accuse them of "having no interest
in extending American culture; indeed, they deny that a
common culture exists. They do not appeal to the common
good, because their idea of community is defined along
racial and ethnic lines. . . . Ethnocentrism tells people that
they must trust and accept only members of their own
group. It breeds hatred and distrust . . . and has no place
in our schools and institutions of higher learning." Beyond
that, Professor Ravitch, echoing others who sincerely seem
to be seeking common ground, goes on to say that "the
cohesive element in the pluralistic approach is the clear
acknowledgment that whatever we are, we are all human.
The thread that binds us is our common humanity, tran-
scending race, color, ethnicity, language, and religion"
(*Chronicle*, 24 October 1991, p. A-44). Place the comments of the PC crowd up against these, and, again, what
is underscored is the divisive nature of the whole PC
business.

Professor Everette Dennis of Columbia seems to be in agreement when he says, "What a shame it would be if the genuine public purpose inherent in multiculturalism were denigrated by racial and ethnic pettiness as now seems quite possible in various disputes." He then goes on to make the very significant and, perhaps, most important observation of this entire discussion. "Of course, East Europeans know a lot about this from a different perspective. . . . After all, among the first *multicultural* societies were their own and they mostly failed" (*War of Words*, p. 7-8). In other words, multi*racial*—Always; multi*cultural*—Never!

Furthermore, it occurs to me that while "we're . . . in danger of forgetting that the Western tradition has been the great liberating tradition in history, the source of ideals of individual freedom and political democracy to which most of the world now aspires," we're also overlooking or perhaps conveniently forgetting the fact that many, if not most, of the cultures being held up by the PC multiculturalists for study and admiration are some of the most oppressive, sexist, misogynistic, patriarchal societies on the planet today. And, while the PC crowd may be able to point to *some* accomplishments of these cultures, they remain, for the most part, primitive as well. An interesting irony to say the least.

Not only is the PNC crowd on campus speaking out more and more, they are even getting organized in their challenge to their PC counterparts. One example of such efforts is the fledgling National Association of Scholars (N.A.S.). As mentioned in chapter 4, the N.A.S. was formed "to promote the study of Western culture and offer a forum to professors who have felt inhibited from questioning affirmative-action programs, required courses on ethnic diversity, and other issues whose advocates are increasingly being described as 'politically correct'" (*Chronicle*, 12 December 1990, p. A-1). The association also "complains that minority professors are paid more, solely because of their race" (*Chronicle*, p. A-16). Professor Dennis points out, I think correctly, that "the letter of the law on matters like affirmative action, anti-harassment, and other socially desirable initiatives long ago outdistanced the spirit of the law and the rationale behind rules that were offered up to improve the quality of life [for some], [were] not [intended] to inflict constraints on all [the rest] of us" (*War of Words*, p. 12).

The National Association of Scholars, although barely four years old, already has statewide affiliates in seventeen states and chapters in twenty-three. It holds national conferences, publishes a journal (*Academic Questions*) and a quarterly newsletter, and, in 1990, the organization gave an award to James S. Coleman, professor of sociology at the University of Chicago, "for resisting efforts to suppress research considered by many sociologists to be 'politically incorrect'" (*Chronicle*, 21 November 1990, p. A-14).

The N.A.S. is based at Princeton University, and its president, Steven H. Balch, said, "There was an initial self-selection for people who considered themselves conservative, but recently people have come to us and said, 'I'm a liberal and a Democrat.'" Case in point, Theodore S. Hamerow, a professor of Central European history at the University of Wisconsin, who admits that he voted for George McGovern for president in 1972, joined the N.A.S. because he was "tired of being bullied by colleagues, students, and administrators whose political agendas have tainted scholarship, the curriculum, faculty-hiring policies, and the campus climate in general" (*Chronicle*, 12 December 1990, p. A-1). James David Barber, professor of political science and policy studies at Duke, joined the N.A.S. because he was concerned that soon no one would even "be able to discuss black or women's studies without being called racist or sexist" (*Chronicle*, 21 November 1990, p. A-14). Professor Barber, by the way, is a former chairman of the board of directors of Amnesty International U.S.A. and describes himself as a "liberal Democrat." Sterling Fishman, a professor of history and education at the University of Wisconsin, also surprised colleagues when he joined the N.A.S. When Michael C. Hinden, a professor of English and a colleague of Fishman's, learned that Professor Fishman, who "isn't exactly known as a conservative," had joined the N.A.S., Professor Hinden said, "I'm still amazed when I learn that people I admire are drawn to its membership" (*Chronicle*, 12 December 1990, p. A-16). Professor Hamerow said, "We have to be prepared to be dubbed racists, fascists, sexists, and reactionaries." But he "adds defiantly, 'We're not an organization of extremists. I'm not going to keep defending myself'" (*Chronicle*, 12 December 1990, p. A-1).

N.A.S. President Stephen H. Balch says, "It's now a matter of talking about tactics rather than simply trying to catch the attention of the rest of the academic world" (*Chronicle*, 30 October 1991, p. A-17). Glenn Ricketts, research director of the N.A.S., said, "Publicity has been one of our most potent weapons." This has mostly involved getting information to alumni regarding troubling changes or directions at the universities. "Alumni awareness is important because many schools, particularly private schools, depend on alumni contributions. When contributions fall off in response to campus shenanigans, school administrators quickly get the message." Ricketts cites Georgetown University's law school dropping an affirmative action policy after that policy "came under fire" as an example of the effectiveness of using alumni awareness to combat PC "campus shenanigans" (*Citizen*, 21 October 1991, p. 15).

The Madison Center is another example of the PNC forces organizing themselves to counter PC and all its "isms" on campus. The center was founded by the University of Chicago's Allan Bloom and former Education Secretary William Bennett "to promote traditional values in the humanities." Even though it got off to a "shaky start," the center is now "back on its feet, said its president, Chester E. Finn, a professor of education and public policy at Vanderbilt University. Its next project is an academic guide to colleges. The center also operates a network for student newspapers founded to provide an alternative—more conservative—voice to mainstream student publications" (*Chronicle*, 30 January 1991, p. A-16).

The Madison Center also sponsored a conference in 1991 the title of which was "Alone, All Alone? The American Campus in a World of Western Resurgence." Speakers, which included John Silber, Lynne V. Cheney, and William Ratliff, a senior research fellow at the Hoover Institution at Stanford, took aim at the PC crowd, and let 'em have it. Lynne Cheney, chairman of the National Endowment for the Humanities and the keynote speaker at the conference, said it was "a pleasure to be with people who have resisted intellectual trendiness . . . who have been willing to be 'politically incorrect' [PNC]." In her keynote address, Cheney called it an "inescapable irony" when, on a recent trip to [what was] the Soviet Union, she kept "hearing again and again about the importance of depoliticizing and deideologizing the study of culture when so often in the United States I hear about the importance of using the arts and the humanities as instruments of politics" (*Chronicle*, 30 January 1991, p. A-15).

President Silber of Boston University abandoned all politeness and admonished PNC professors not to be "so civil" and "so cordial," but to "subject [PC scholars] to the ridicule they so richly deserve." Adding his voice to Silber's call to arms, Professor Ratliff accused "the majority" of being "silent," therefore "abdicating its responsibility" and allowing "the minority [to] gain the upper hand." Ratliff also maintained that a "good scholar" is one who is willing to "allow the evidence to convince you you're wrong" (*Chronicle*, 30 January 1991, p. A-16).

Yet another development in the battle against PC has been the creation of the American Association for the Advancement of Core Curriculum, the purpose of which is to convince educators of the value of a core curriculum, of which a "canon" would be an integral part. Carl A. Raschke, a professor of religious studies at the University of Denver and head of Denver's Institute for the Humanities, was the founding president of the association which "intends to serve as a clearinghouse—and cheerleader— for professors and administrators who want to create more coherent general education programs for undergraduates" and asserts that "revival of interest in the core is the most important movement in education of the last 15 or 20 years." Professor Raschke "says [that] he has little tolerance for other scholars who want to promote strict, politicized viewpoints," and that "he's worried that no one cares about giving undergraduates a sensible education" (*Chronicle*, 9 January 1991, p. A-3).

This is also a critical development for elementary and secondary education for as E. D. Hirsch, author of *Cultural Literacy*, contends in an unpublished essay entitled "Fairness and Core Knowledge," all the information we have indicates that the students who perform best in international academic competitions come from countries which have curricula which are very specific about a body of "core knowledge that teachers are responsible for teaching and kids are responsible for learning." Education systems which specify in detail the material students are expected to learn "enable tutors to focus on the specific knowledge that students need in order to attain grade level." This "specified material" in the humanities is a canon, which is what the PC crowd continues to attack. So, according to the available statistical information and evidence, the politically correct movement toward multicultural approaches and *away* from the "canonical great books approach," so widespread today at all levels of public education, is movement in *exactly* the *wrong* direction. Still, in the United States the material that is studied at different grade levels remains, for the most part, a matter of local choice, and this is a major part of the problem.

Based on this information, the *Excellence in Education* seminar, which I attended during the 1988 Republican National Convention in New Orleans, came to the conclusion that the United States needs to establish national standards for education based on international norms. It is critical that international norms be considered because our kids will have to compete on a global level, not a local one, if they are to be successful in the world of tomorrow. And, to ascertain whether or not those standards are being met, we must test our kids at regular intervals and link promotion to performance, which we stopped doing in the late sixties and early seventies. Many educators link this move to the advent of court-ordered busing, but the reason, at this point, is irrelevant. What matters is that we fix it.

As pointed out in chapter 2, the argument that we do not spend enough money on education or that spending on education has been cut simply has no basis in fact. The problem is not how much we spend, but *how* we spend. We spend far too much money, for instance, on administration and not nearly enough in the classroom. Spending money "in the classroom" means buying instructional materials, reducing teacher/pupil ratios, and enhancing teacher salaries. Under the present system, there are economic incentives for good teachers to get out of the classroom because administrators' salaries are higher than those of teachers.

If teacher salaries are to be increased, however, taxpayers want and are entitled to some assurance that they will get a decent return for their investment. To be perfectly frank, there are many teachers in the classroom today who simply are not qualified to be there. That is the fault of the universities because these individuals have received degrees from institutions of higher education. By and large, these individuals will have degrees in education, and, almost to a person, teachers who I know and respect say that a degree in education is really not worth very much. Yet, according to present certification methods, a person with a degree in secondary education, regardless of his or her emphasis, is considered more qualified to teach biology in high school than a person with a master's degree in biology. Sound crazy? Consider this.

In order to teach in the state of Louisiana, one must be "certified in education." I hold a Ph.D. in English, and I have been teaching composition, literature, and creative writing for over fifteen years, and, according to the standards of certification in this state, I am considered unqualified to teach English to seniors in high school because I do not have a bachelor's degree in education and have never passed the National Teachers Exam (the NTE). Yet, under present certification methods, someone with a bachelor's degree in Physical Education is considered qualified to teach English, history, math, or any other subject in high school. This is absurd by *any* standard of rational analysis. Such certification processes must be altered and at least brought into line with common sense, as they were in Tennessee. In addition, the quality of the programs which train our teachers must be reevaluated, and some of those programs should be discontinued.

Again, as mentioned in chapter 2, educational reform is needed in five specific areas: 1) administration; 2) instruction; 3) curriculum; 4) testing; and 5) values.

1) At the administrative level, we must reduce the number of administrative positions and the salaries of these positions. We must also require that administrators teach at least part-time. The purpose of this proposal is to provide economic incentives for our best teachers to stay *in the classroom* where they belong and where they are needed.

2) At the instructional level, we must revise certification processes so that teachers in the middle- and high-school level will be required to have degrees in the disciplines in which they teach rather than in education. Furthermore, a person with a master's degree or higher in a particular discipline should be automatically certified in that discipline and in that discipline only. Teacher/pupil

ratios must be reduced, which can be accomplished, in part, if administrators go back into the classroom at least part-time. Teacher salaries must be made competitive with other professions so that we can attract qualified people into the classroom. If the administrative reforms are implemented, some of this could actually be done without increasing spending. Teachers must also understand that they will be held accountable for teaching kids, which brings us to the next area of concern.

3) In the area of curriculum, we simply must establish a core curriculum, "a body of core knowledge," as Hirsch calls it, which we must then expect our teachers to teach and our students to learn. This core curriculum, which must have a "canon" and stress the development of basic skills, will be our national standard, and it should be based on international norms. Teachers must also be held to strict accountability based on the performance of their class, as a whole, on standardized tests which should measure the class's familiarity with and mastery of the core.

4) Before going into the area of testing, it is important to emphasize that teachers should only be held accountable for the performance of the class *as a whole*. It would be unfair to hold a teacher responsible for every single one of his or her students because, as it was once put, sometimes the reason Johnny can't read is because Johnny is a jerk. In order to be fair, each class would have to be tested twice, once at the beginning of the school year to determine its performance level, and then again at the end of the year to measure its progress. To be sure, not every student will do well, and some will fail. That is to be expected. But if the entire class is performing below the norms, then something must be done with that teacher. If additional training doesn't correct the situation, then dismissal would be in order.

Such a system will allow teachers to maintain complete autonomy in their classrooms, so long as they are doing their jobs. In other words, whatever pedagogical techniques a teacher chooses to use to accomplish his or her goals does not matter. What matters is that the goals be achieved, and the goals should be the same for all. If one reading teacher takes a traditional approach by having students sit in neat rows of desks and read aloud, so be it. If another wants to take his or her students outside to swing from the trees while reading Edgar Rice Boroughs, so be that too, as long as *all* those students learn to read.

5) In the area of values, and this will send the PC crowd into an absolute lather, the education establishment must finally abandon the absurd notion of "value-free" education. Now that is *not* to say that teachers are free to stand in front of a class full of students and say things like: "Think as I think; I am Catholic, so you must be Catholic; I am a Democrat; so you must be a Democrat." They should not and must not do this. But, teachers can and must once again say to their students things like: "Lying is wrong; cheating is wrong; stealing is wrong; doing drugs is wrong and dangerous, and so is promiscuous sex, and these things will *not* be tolerated in our schools." And the deconstructionist claim that these terms are relative must stop.

As for the parents of students, you've heard it all before. Get involved. Ask questions. Visit your children's schools. Ask questions. Talk to your children's teachers. Ask questions. Look at your kids' textbooks and see if they contain any "facts" that shock you. If so, ask questions. Ask questions anyway. If your kids are learning more in their history class about the internment of Japanese-Americans during World War II than about the major military campaigns of that war, demand to know why, which is *not* to say that they should not learn about Japanese-American internment at all. Ask to see the books they are assigned to read in their English classes. Be informed; don't be shy; ask questions.

If you are a college-age student or will be one soon, be prepared for what you will find. Most people find the university intimidating. That's fine; it is and should be an awe-inspiring place. Most people also find college professors intimidating. Again, that is a perfectly reasonable reaction. People who are teaching in college have advanced degrees and should be treated with the appropriate deference and respect. Besides, they give the grades. If you have been raised on traditional values, you should expect to encounter people who will have hostile attitudes toward you and who will belittle those values you have been taught, and some of those people will be professors. While you must always be respectful of faculty, you do not have to tolerate ridicule. You must, of course, be careful for two reasons.

First of all, you are in college to learn about things that you do not already know, and you may well learn things that surprise you; in fact, that *should* happen. So do not assume that a professor is merely expressing a political point of view simply because he or she says something with which you do not agree or that you find unusual. Secondly, as already pointed out, any person who is teaching in college obviously has more education than you do and deserves that respect, and you should never challenge a professor's competence in front of his or her class. But, if any professor makes a point that really strikes you as outlandish, you have every right to question that professor, but not to be disrespectful or belligerent, which may mean going to the professor's office after class. If the professor is at all evasive when you inquire about the nature of the evidence and where you can find it, you would then be justified in questioning the validity of what you have been told. If you feel intimidated about asking questions, then drop the class and take it at another time with another professor who you find to be more open-minded and with whom you are more comfortable. Remember, as Dr. Marotta pointed out, "the great number of American academics occupy a rational middle ground."

There are times, however, when a student really

doesn't regard dropping a class as an acceptable alternative. Sometimes, you may find yourself so far into a semester that you won't want to start over again. Some classes are difficult to get into, and some are offered only once a year instead of every semester. Students who are getting close to the end of their college career also may not be able to drop and start over. If you do decide to stay in a class in which you feel the instructor is prejudiced, then the only advice I can give you is to practice common-sense survival techniques. While there are appeal processes available, remember, the professor gives the grade.

There are ways to avoid professors with whom you might be uncomfortable. All students are assigned an advisor. Share your concerns with that person. If you find a professor that you like, you might also seek his or her advice. But, most professors have never had classes with each other, therefore we have no first-hand knowledge of each other as teachers. Most of us are also reluctant to speak of any of our colleagues in a negative way. So, the best advice about how teachers teach will come from your peers, other students who have actually taken classes with those professors.

Chapter 7

INTERVIEWS

The first interview is with Dr. Gary Marotta, professor of history and Academic Vice-President of the University of Southwestern Louisiana.

DT: I want to ask you about a statement you made which I have already quoted in the book. You said, "In the 1950s the right-wingers were trying to close the door to liberals. Now the other side is trying to close the door." That was in the *Vermilion*, July 26, 1990.

Marotta: Yeah, that's right. I think that's the one where the reporter asked me about cultural diversity/cultural pluralism. All I know is that within weeks of that interview coming out, I was stopped by at least five faculty members and three students wanting to know why I was espousing this racist point of view.

DT: Do you think your point of view is racist?

Marotta: No. I believe that we are members of Western civilization, and we have to know the values and beliefs and ideas of our own civilization even before we can comprehend another's, and even when we try to understand another people's perspectives and views of the world, it's going to be filtered through our own beliefs anyway. I also think it is important that an American read and understand the *Federalist Papers* before they read the thoughts of Mao Tse Tung because they need a baseline which is their own from which to compare things because Western tradition has an extraordinary ability to draw in ideas from other cultures that already resonate in our own culture. It's a highly selective process, but you have to understand your own ideas first, and if you don't, I think you're defenseless.

You don't know who you are or where you're coming from. During the 1960s, there was a resurgence in mystical thinking, and Western civilization was criticized for being *homologicus* and we were missing an important spiritual dimension of life. Well, it's as though they had no familiarity with the Western world of the Greeks and the Romans and obviously the Judeo-Christian tradition, which is rich with mystical thought. Suddenly we all felt that we all had to be Hindus or Buddhists or maybe a Taoist because we simply did not know what was in our own tradition because we had abandoned it. It wasn't being taught. The obligation of one generation passing on the cultural heritage had been dismantled during the so-called reforms of the 1960s, which involved the abandonment of the old core curriculum and the abandonment of the history of the ideas of Western civilization.

DT: I would like to read something to you and let you respond to it. [I then read the excerpts from the column in the *Vermilion* which is about Christianity being a "key element" being used to "keep African-American minds in bondage" and which states that "the real Son of God was black and born 4000 years before Jesus" see chap. 3)] How do you respond to that?

Marotta: Two things. One, a matter of historical fact, the second, a matter of simple logic. The historical fact is that the evolution of slavery in colonial America was gradual. The first evidence we have of blacks coming to the colonies is in 1619, one year before the arrival of the Mayflower. Those blacks did not come as slaves. They came in a category of "unfreedom," close to indentured servitude. Slavery, as it developed, did not exist then. Those Africans came here, as did most Europeans, in a status of "unfreedom." The development of slavery is very subtle, and the case for racism in Western culture in the seventeenth-century cannot be made. It involves labor, and it codifies much later with the advent much later of slavery in the nineteenth-century and is resurrected again in the late nineteenth-century with ideological racist thought. So

those statements you read are "ahistorical" or "unhistorical."
Secondly, there is such a thing called a contradiction. One
can't have both sides of that argument. One cannot say
that blacks are brainwashed by white, European Christianity and at the same time argue that the source of European
Christianity is Africa. You can't have it both ways. And
if all things good are African and all things bad are European, we have a lot of explaining to do. There's a big
logical hole there that most people would call a contradiction.

DT: Schlesinger is saying basically the same thing.

Marotta: Look, there's no question that we had slavery,
and that slavery and racism went together. There is also
no question that Americans recognized that slavery went
against their own professions and against their own ideological premises. That's why the Civil War was fought.
And that was within America; that was a *civil* war, and
it was a war because Americans, black and white, thought
that slavery was antithetical to American beliefs. It was
that same contradiction that forced Americans to face up
to the civil rights issues of the fifties, sixties, and seventies.
Martin Luther King understood fully that to win he would
have to take the moral highground on American ideology
and quote to America, as Frederick Douglas and many
others had, of the existence of that contradiction and leave
it to the American conscience and the guilt of the American
people to make right their historic wrong. There's no
denying the wrongs, but it is also a mistake to think that
no whites were for civil rights or against slavery. They
joined with blacks to fight for American ideals. What won
the civil rights struggle was America, and you don't hear
Martin Luther King talking about black power. Martin
Luther King understood about moral ideals, and I think
he understood that the call for black power would have
only led to the call for white power, and he never made
that mistake. He always kept the alliance with whites as
Americans. I think it's no accident that after his death and
with the advent of black power, that things fell apart.

DT: In an article that you sent me you used the word "multicultural" which surprised me because it was an early article.

Marotta: That was early seventies.

DT: Right. And you said that misconceptions spawned by pluralism were distorting educational policy. Do you think that politically correct multiculturalism is distorting educational policy today?

Marotta: Yes. I think there's no question. I think that what I pointed to as a potential problem has actualized itself. It leads to notions like Afrocentristic studies. It leads to separate departments of this and that particular ethnic or interest group. These areas merit study, but they should be infused into the existing curricula and should not be ghetto-ized. We are reinventing ethnic and racial apartheid, and it's a mistake. Behind it, I think, is a group's search for power and not the individual quest for truth. They want their own department, their own budget, and everything else, and I think it's very dangerous, and we can see the extreme manifestations of it all around us, and I think it's antithetical to the pursuit of inquiry.

DT: Would you include gay and lesbian studies in that?

Marotta: Yes. No question about it.

DT: Again, I was amazed at some of the issues you covered in that early piece because they're so salient and relevant today.

Marotta: In those days, all these things sounded like wonderful things. I wrote that piece because I was very worried about where they could conceivably go. I think you can tell from that article, it's like when Richard Wright felt that he had to break away from the Communist party because they wanted to impose their will on how he wrote literature. And I was seeing things then that led me to think that even though this was supposed to be a good, positive move, that they were moving in very exclusive kinds of directions and that they were moving into a lot of danger, that there were serious, potential problems.

DT: I have perceived that there is a wet blanket being

thrown on this whole discussion by people who either say that this discussion is not scholarly or who call others racist for bringing up points that are not considered "politically correct."

Marotta: That's definitely happening. As I said earlier, it happened to me. It's worse than even an *ad hominem* argument because it's ascribing motivations instead of facing the ideas and the substance of the argument. It's phony. It's absolute nonsense, absolute nonsense.

DT: James Berlin's position [Berlin is a professor from Purdue who had appeared on our campus during the week of this interview] was that this is *the* topic of scholarship right now, that we *must* discuss this whole area of political correctness, multiculturalism, Afrocentrism, etc. What do you think?

Marotta: I agree. This discussion and this debate holds the key to the future of liberal arts education. That's what this debate is about. Which way is it going to go? It's the very heart of the matter. Faculty who shy away from engaging in this issue are ethically irresponsible. This is our job. This is our calling. This is precisely what we ought to be debating. Not to debate this is to say, "I don't care." And if you don't care about this, then you probably shouldn't be in the university. I mean, I don't understand what else you could conceivably care about than issues such as these, the future of the core education of the next generation of intellectuals. Every faculty member from computer science to engineering to English to sociology has to be in this debate. Not to join this debate is to say that you're not fit to be an academic. And if you're not fit to be an academic, that's unethical, and you should leave the university community.

DT: Are you familiar with Stanley Fish?

Marotta: Yes, at Duke.

DT: He said that faculty members who have 'illiberal' attitudes toward multicultural studies and all this should not be allowed to sit on committees which decide tenure and promotion matters.

Marotta: Nonsense.

DT: But this is the head of a department making these statements.

Marotta: I still subscribe to the notion that the great number of American academics command a certain rational middle ground. What's distressing is those with power who propound extreme ideological points of view which can only be defended with the most contorted kinds of logic and which are always attached to some social goal occupy an intellectual hegemony. And they've created a climate that does not allow for rational debate. One is written out, one is excommunicate, one is anathema.

DT: How is it all enforced, all this politically correct thinking?

Marotta: I think it is enforced through peer pressure, perhaps not so much intimidation but the natural desire of human beings to be wanted and to be part of a group. Then you have the notion that because of this exclusivity, I will simply go along with the group and think my private thoughts or I will let myself be intellectually bullied.

DT: Do you think it's enforced through tenure or promotion?

Marotta: There are dogmatists who have used tenure and promotion to enforce it. People who cannot see the difference. They are dangerous people, very dangerous people. Those people are the same as the McCarthyites of the fifties only they dress up in their liberal humanitarian garb, but there is no difference. There are certain meanings that are never justifiable, and you never use the instruments of promotion and tenure to deny somebody advancement because you don't agree with their ideas. If you don't agree with the ideas because the ideas are invalid, because they are not documented, because they're neurotic ravings, then of course you vote against it. You know, we don't believe that anybody's idea is as good as anybody else's idea. The idea is better because it is better argued, because it is logical, because it is documented. And that's what gives it its power, not the quick rhetorical trick or because it's the popular hula-hoop of the day. That doesn't add legitimacy to it.

DT: Are you familiar with Stephan Thernstrom?

Marotta: Yes, the historian.

DT: He said this sort of atmosphere where a few highly mobilized radical students intimidate everyone else is a new McCarthyism and more frightening than the old because the old had no support within the academy.

Marotta: It's the same as the SDS, in the latter days of the SDS when they went crazy. The early SDS was genuinely students for a democratic society, for democracy, and they became increasingly dogmatic, increasingly a group of zealots who wanted to deny everybody else's belief and everybody else's freedom of speech. They were advocating that PC long before we picked it up from old Marxist Johnny and made it commonplace. It was there before. It'll always be there. It's the witch hunters; it's the same old bunch. There's nothing new to it. It's the old starched proceedings, a counter-reformation, the special organizations that were set up to make sure we were thinking correctly and all that. It's nothing new. It's nothing new. It's the same people who wanted Socrates to take hemlock or who wanted to throw Galileo out of the Church. It's the latest secular version.

DT: One of our colleagues at the Academic Discussion Group the other night said that during the McCarthy Era, people got fired, and we're not having that now, and I said that's not true. The number of professors is quite large and growing who have at least claimed to have been denied tenure, promotion, been fired for expressing racist opinions . . .

Marotta: Alleged racist opinion.

DT: Exactly. Or "illiberal," a word Stanley Fish uses.

Marotta: Yeah, he means anyone whose opinions disagree with his. I hear the same thing; I don't know that they're that widespread. I really don't. I think there may be some truth in it, but to think that it dominates is, I think, incorrect.

DT: Do you believe in the core?

Marotta: Yes. You mean the core curriculum?

DT: Yes. What should be on it?

Marotta: Yes, and I think we should have a canon at USL. I think we should start off with reading great literature as faculty identify it and believe in it. If you don't believe in it, then you believe in absolutely nothing. Each of us— I've had this discussion with faculty members here who did not want to have a prescribed, defined core curriculum. I'd ask them what their favorite course is—and I would say, "Do you assign readings?" And they would say, "Yes." And I would say, "Why do you assign them?" And they would say, "This is what you have to know." And I said, "Isn't there something you have to know to be an educated person?" And the problem is you have a consensus about what that is. If the academic vice-president were the same as an academic dictator, which it obviously is not, I could go home tonight and put together a complete syllabus with the prescribed readings that I think would be appropriate to U.S.-educated students. I could do it in one evening. I know exactly what I think. I dare to play a role and say, "Look, let's not beg the question, there is a body of knowledge out there, there are books we ought to be reading." I'll say, "Here's what I think. If you want to change it, go ahead."

DT: What would you say to those who say we couldn't come up with a consensus?

Marotta: Then we come up with the best respectable estimate.

DT: I think we can.

Marotta: I think we can, too.

DT: What do we say to those who say we can't?

Marotta: I think we give it our best shot. Not to come up with it is to beg the question; it's to capitulate; it's to fail in our obligation to define what students ought to know. That's our obligation. In the 1960s, the great mistake was that students thought they had the right to dictate to the faculty what they should know and what they should read. And the shame of the professoriate is that they capitulated to the students. There's a presumption in education, and the presumption is that the trained intellect of the faculty knows better than the untutored intellect of the student, and they come to us to learn because, ostensibly, we know something. Now if we can't define what we know, then you have very bad faculty. We must define that. It's logic. When Burton Raffel brought that scholar from the New School social research here a few weeks ago, Eli Sagan, in his talk he said something very interesting. He said he does not subscribe to the notion of PC, but he does subscribe to the notion of LC—logically correct. And I subscribe to that, too.

DT: One of the things that's being tossed around in history—that's your particular field—is this notion that history cannot be objective, history is nothing but half-truths. There's a certain part of me that understands where that's coming from. On the other hand, when you move into the area of history as half-truths and you cannot be objective, how do you challenge a David Duke who questions the holocaust. I don't see how you can.

Marotta: Those who advocate that position are the historical equivalents of the literary critics who subscribe to deconstructionism. They say, "There is no truth," and, "We can never know truth wholly." I think we recognize, particularly in the humanities and the social sciences, that we can never fully grasp truth objectively because we cannot get outside of our biography, we cannot fully get outside of our culture, we cannot fully get outside of our biases, "I am male; I am white; I am ethnic immigrant; I am urban"—that's going to shape a lot of my thinking. But we have to believe that there is an objective reality which has a way of impinging itself on our consciousness, and we have to maintain—it's not a myth—we have to maintain the belief in truth and our struggle is to approximate truth and objectivity as best we can apprehend it, and when an error in logic or in substance or in documentation is called to our attention, it's our duty to correct it even if it does not fit with the conclusion we were coming to or the ideology we subscribe to. We must believe in truth and we must believe in objectivity even though we know we cannot fully describe it or fully achieve it. To say there is none, then that gives merit to the notion that everything can be manipulated, and that anything can be said, and it opens the relativistic arguments that my truth is as good as your truth and who's to say it's not true.

DT: John Silber said that the crisis on the American campus today, insofar as there is one, has to do with what he calls the "profound relativism" which has taken root.

Marotta: There is something to be said for relativistic arguments. It's important that in writing the history, for example, of the South, and telling the story from the point of view of the "big house," and that captures a dimension of history. It's important for someone who has empathy with the slave quarters to tell the story from that vantage point too, insofar as you can. But the scholar who tells it from the point of view of the "big house," once it's called to his attention, has to deal with the fact that the social dialectic of southern history had to do with the interplay of all quarters on the plantation, and there was a world that the slave owners shaped, and there was a world that the slave shaped, and you have to see it that way. To understand even the Marxist point of view of the class struggle, you cannot just see it from the point of view of the working class. You must understand it from the point of view of the so-called ruling class as well. And that's why a first-rate southern scholar will say to the world, "Don't dismiss any point of view, whether you agree with it or not." Finally, there is an objective reality, and you have to read all of it, the slave owners and the slave narratives, to get at it.

DT: Now, I would call that a *true* multicultural approach.

Marotta: But that's not multicultural. Multicultural now is "just my point of view."

DT: Yes. And, as I have encountered it, multiculturalism has an agenda which is not only to exclude the point of view of the white, western Europeans, it is to vilify that group. In other words, not only is it regarded as not worth considering, it's worse than that; it's a source of evil, of corruption, of all the misery and sufferings of humanity.

Marotta: That's right. The history department at a university where I taught decided to have a course in Afro-American history. The chairman of the department turned to a black member of the department and said, "Well, that's it. You work up the course." That faculty member turned to him, as someone who loved the chairman of the department, and said, "I don't know anything about African-American history. Finally it's a cognitive issue. Simply because I'm black doesn't mean I know anything about it."

DT: There seems to be something racist about assuming that.

Marotta: Absolutely. And, the person who made the assumption is not a racist, but yes, there is something racist about assuming it, or at least there's something political about it. In other words, I think the chairman wanted this person to teach the course because he was black, and he understood that this was more than just the search for truth, that this was a statement that black students wanted black history, that it said something about black power, that they wanted a black person to teach it because he was a role model, *ad infinitum*. Okay? But this faculty member had the good sense to say, "Look, the person in this department who knows more about this subject than anybody else is Gary Marotta, and so he should teach it." And the question did come up that I was white. And, he said, 'Yeah, but, I have a Ph.D. from the University of Chicago in the history of the French Enlightenment, and I would be shocked if anyone in this department told me that I couldn't teach

that because my ancestry is African instead of French. Or
if a bunch of French students on campus said, 'We don't
want him to teach that course because he's not French.'"
And that's the whole issue right there. I was teaching a
course, and there was this fellow in the class who said he
was a black Muslim, and he decided to wage the campaign
that a white person cannot teach the soul of the black
people, and he was tremendously disruptive. I finally went
to the library and got an issue of *Mein Kampf* and selected
a particularly vitriolic passage, and wherever he said Jew
or Slav or Gypsy, I put in white, and wherever he put in
Aryan or German, I put in black, and I read it. And he
loved it. Then I showed them the book, and this guy came
up to me after class and said, "I owe you an apology."

DT: That speaks well of him.

Marotta: It speaks very well of him, but it took
that kind of shock. He never for a moment believed that
what he was saying was profoundly racist. Again, this is
a cognitive discipline, and you master it by learning it, and
just because you come from a certain background, that
doesn't give you a grasp of it. You must be a student of
it, a scholar of it. Here's the whole issue when it comes
to cultural diversity and multiculturalism in terms of the
American experience. We should not have "group think."
Group think can only mean a party line, and there should
only be the primacy of the thought of the individual. Groups
can be effective in political action for civil rights and
economic justice, but one only becomes a successful busi-
nessman by doing it and achieving it on one's own. You
only become a successful scholar by doing it by yourself.
Groups can't do that. It just doesn't happen. It's as dangerous to have group think in academics as it is in the world.
I think one of the benefits of American civilization is the
notion of the primacy of the individual. And that is the
sphere of civil rights protecting us. And that's reinforced
in America with academic freedom within the academic
community. And it is dangerous to the pursuit of truth to

have group conformity imposed on that. As a matter of fact, the idea of group conformity and group think, whether it's white group, Italian group, lesbian group, black group, I don't care what it is, it's all there in de Tocqueville's *Democracy in America.* One of the dangers he saw was the notion of democracy coming into conflict with the equally prevailing American belief in the primacy of the individual, and that's the potential conflict. And the principal job is to reconcile democracy with the notion of the primacy of the individual. And that's the issue of cultural pluralism versus shared set of academic beliefs and versus the primacy of the intellect of the individual.

DT: Your friend, Professor Dennis?

Marotta: Yeah, at Columbia.

DT: Right. In his talk that you sent me, he made the point that no "multicultural" society has ever succeeded. You can have multiracial societies, but not multicultural.

Marotta: Of course. Multicultural means you have no society.

DT: I guess the question is this: Is there an American society, an American culture, which is different from any other on this planet, and that, *ipso facto*, you and I have more in common with black women, say, in this country, than they do with black women in Africa?

Marotta: No question about it. That's absolutely true. There was a friend of mine—I knew her back in the seventies—she's now the president of a major university in New Jersey. She went to Africa to find her roots and all that, and she came back with a profound appreciation of herself as an American, and when she went there for the second time, she said, "I'm taking my mink." We're Americans; that's what we are. We all have something distinct about us because we're born into certain circumstances. We're born into a certain religion; we're born into a certain ethnic background; we're born into a certain social class. Having said all of that, to say that you're not overwhelmingly American is utter nonsense. And we have more

in common with what defines us as Americans than with
what defines us as subsets. We are a cultural unit, and part
of what defines our cultural unity is that we subscribe to
a set of beliefs which we all should believe are politically
correct. Those beliefs are contained in our great state
papers: the Declaration of Independence, the Constitution,
the Gettysburg Address, and it's about democracy, and it's
about the primacy of the individual, it's about the American
mission in the world, it's about civil rights, it's about
justice. And when you put it all together, America is an
idea.

The next interview is with Burton Raffel, distinguished
professor of literature and humanities at USL. Dr. Raffel
is also a lawyer and has taught in the law school at the
University of Denver.

DT: Are you familiar with the so-called politically
correct movement?
Raffel: Oh boy, am I familiar with it—unfortunately.
DT: Tell me what you think it is.
Raffel: I think it is a number of things, but at the heart
of it is power. In the old days, if you were staging a coup,
if you were taking over somebody else's castle, for example, you'd take his keys away, you know, so you had
control over what was going on. What is going on now
with this political correctness is they're not only taking
the keys away, they're changing the locks and sometimes
they're burning down the building. Look what's happening
at the University of Syracuse. The entire undergraduate
English program at this major university has been quote
revamped to suit the modernist / post-modernist ideas of
things, and the traditional English curriculum in which you
read dull and boring things like plays and poems and stories
and novels has been eliminated, and now you have courses
in critical approaches and ethnocentricities and so forth
and so forth, and you do read a couple of these traditional,
boring things as illustrations and artifacts and so forth, but

mostly what you read, and honestly, I wish I were making this up, mostly what you read are the critical writings of these people.

DT: And the traditional, boring things to which you refer are mostly written by dead, white guys, right?

Raffel: Most of them, yeah, of course. Dead white males, yes. It's incredible. It's just incredible to see the power of this. Look, you always have change, and the younger people come in and throw the older people out, and you go from the "old criticism" to the "new criticism" . . . and things change and people see things differently, but the major difference between this and what has gone before is not only that they're, as I say, changing the locks and sometimes burning down the buildings, but this is also associated with a whole development after World War II, and it's particularly strong in the United States. I mean the French "BS" [deconstruction] comes from France, but we take it and smear it all over our faces and say, "Gee, aren't we great." It's absolutely incredible to see what we do with this. This is associated with a whole movement of, one could call it, contempt, dissaffection, distaste for traditional values, dislike of the United States of America, which is very fashionable. One idea that goes along with the whole PC movement is to constantly put down the United States and say how much better other cultures are, how much better other people are, how much better other governmental systems are when they don't know a damned thing about these other things. I've had discussions with people about the defects, for example, in the American judicial system, and they're real, I admit, but after listening to a certain amount of that, I say, "Wait a minute. Let's put this in perspective. Let's take one of these foreign cultures that you make a lot of noise about and compare them." To have any kind of sanity and rational balance you must compare what's *actually* going on here with what's actually going on elsewhere. And it's the same thing in literature. Two books come to mind which illustrate this point beautifully. I saw a book published by the

University of Chicago Press, very reputable press, and it was a book on the "actual facts of publication." It was about the economics of publishing and the relationships between publishers and authors, and this is extremely important, as you know. And I bought this book, which was very expensive, and it came, and it was very small, and I started reading it, and it was worthless. The reason it was worthless is because it started with this whole notion that the modern world, particularly as we in the West represent it, is no good. They assume axiomatically, *a priori*, class conflicts at every level, whether there are class conflicts or not. I mean, if you're dealing with Anthony Trollope dealing with his publishers, there is no class conflict. I mean, that is absolute nonsense. There is no foundation for that whatsoever. Yet, this is a matter of dogma and doctrine for them, and so what they will start doing is fabricating the truth, fabricating, quote facts, making things up and saying things that I know as a matter of plain, sober fact are not true, but it corresponds with their theory.

DT: These are academics?

Raffel: Academics, yes, published by the University of Chicago Press. I did a seminar on sixteenth-century English poetry, and you'd think that by the time you got back to the sixteenth-century that maybe these people wouldn't be such idiots. Because I made that assumption, I made the mistake of buying a similar book on sixteenth-century poetry, and the book is again virtually useless. It starts off talking about class conflict at the court of Henry VIII. I mean, you've got to be virtually insane to talk about that. I mean, sure there was tension between the king and the nobles, but to talk of that as class conflict is not even Marxist; it's garbage.

DT: Do you associate those kinds of things with deconstruction?

Raffel: Oh yeah, sure. The deconstructionist approach is basically an approach characterized by dissaffection with the way we do things. Our words don't mean anything,

our books don't mean anything; so we can have contempt
for everything, and everybody is motivated by power
because we're motivated by power. I mean, that's their
attitude. So you can bend and twist anything and everything. This, to me, is not at all scholarly.

DT: Is deconstruction where it all begins?

Raffel: I think the intellectual tendencies start before
that, but I think the intellectual roots of it are in France.

DT: Before Derrida?

Raffel: Oh, Derrida. You know, I've read one book
of Derrida, and that's all I could take. Now, I very carefully
chose a book in which he was being interviewed because
I figured this would be easier to take than the full stream,
and I found out something very interesting. Derrida is a
very sensitive and a very smart man, but he's a human
being. He was in a session with American academics, and
he would say these things that were, you know, 90 percent
true, and they would accept it as gospel, you know, this
is God talking. And the next statement he would make
would be 80 percent true, and the reaction was the same.
And the next statement was 60 percent true, you know.
He could get away with saying anything, and no matter
what idiocy he would throw out, they would say, "Oh, gee,
that's marvelous." And their brains had just turned to mush.
And the French, of course, are very good at this. In French,
if you say something elegantly enough, it doesn't matter
if it's true or not. And French BS is a characteristic of it,
and the French learn to discount it, but American academics
take it all so seriously.

DT: And you think that deconstruction goes further
back than Derrida?

Raffel: I would go back to [Jean-Paul] Sartre. I think
there's a lot of that kind of thing in Sartre, not in Camus,
but certainly in Sartre. In his late 1930s novel *La Nausee*,
the basic argument and the emotional proposition is that
our Western existence is nothing, that we are nothing; we
are no good; our lives are no good; there is no point to

it; we are disgusting, and life is disgusting, and everything is disgusting. And that makes a certain amount of sense in 1939 with Hitler in the world and Stalin in the world. But after World War II, people continue in this mode which eventually leads to what we now call deconstruction, and Sartre has a lot to do with it, with the disassociation of human beings from the world in which they live, and it's not just fashionable Marxists. This mentality finally corrupts, not simply the university structures, nor simply the intellectual structures, but more importantly it corrupts the moral structures. One of the things that these people don't want to understand is that the very basis of social cohesion is an agreed upon set of values which we call morality, and if people *don't* operate *morally*, those social structures break down. I did an interview with a young Ph.D. on translation, and I said to him, which struck him like a bolt out of the blue, that one of my major motives, if not *the* major motive for all the translation work I've done, is a moral issue. I owe a debt to society and to those who have gone before me, which I seek to repay in my work, and the morality of paying back that debt is the whole name of the game. And it was amazing to me that this man had apparently never thought of translation or of writing, in general, as a moral act.

DT: What about teaching?

Raffel: Teaching, of course. A "professor" is one who is supposed to "profess." It's who you are and what you represent in the classroom. But, you should never teach from an ideological point of view or try to make disciples.

DT: So you consider teaching a moral act?

Raffel: It should be.

DT: Then it can also be immoral?

Raffel: Obviously. For example, take the two books I mentioned. As far as I am concerned, *the* basic rule of scholarship and the basic definition of scholarship is telling the truth as closely and as accurately as you can tell it, whether it leads in directions you like or whether it leads in directions you don't like. Telling the truth, truth telling, is absolutely essential. Now, the fact that we, none of us, are God and that we can't establish absolute truth does not mean that we can't come closer to it and that some things aren't truer than others. And people who make up so-called facts or bend facts, whether it is in a political context or not, are immoral. In a scholarly context, there is nothing worse that you can do in the world than lie.

DT: Do you see people in our profession, in the professoriate, doing that today?

Raffel: You know we do. Very interesting aspect of that. I functioned for a while as a dean at the Ontario College of Art, a public institution. It came to my attention that some of the 'artsy-fartsy' professors, that's what I call them, were sufficiently arrogant that they were not attending their classes. I got kind of upset about that, and I said, "Well, they show up on time to get their checks, and I would call that stealing." Now you can break tenure for that, and I would have done it, but I needed evidence. So I made out and distributed some anonymous forms for students to fill out when Professor X and Professor Y were not in class, and do you know how many I got back? None. Not one person who complained would follow through. Now I take that as an indication that the morality was all in the mouth. I mean, they would complain and make noises about something that was clearly wrong, but they would not follow up.

DT: Could professors who meet their classes *not* be doing their job?

Raffel: Obviously. The grounds for breaking tenure are incompetence or immorality. There are all the obvious kinds of incompetence and immorality. I think people who are indoctrinating, from any point of view, in the classroom should not be teaching. I don't care what the position is. These "new left" people, I have no patience with those people. They don't look at reality; they just make noise. As an example, one of my daughters was in an American history class, and I know something about American history; I have written a couple of books in the field. Anyway, she came home and started telling me the things that her high-school teacher was telling her, and he was making up American history. He was very glib and he was very exciting, but he was making it up. Now as far as I am concerned, he should be fired. He should be given the opportunity to correct and reform, I mean, you don't just put him up against the wall and shoot him, but someone who is going to make up American history doesn't belong in a classroom.

DT: There was a "Nightline" program recently focusing on the impact of multiculturalism specifically on the instruction of history. Professor Manning Marable was on that program, and he spoke here at USL this past week as part of the "Eyes Wide Open" program. Let me throw a couple of things at you that he said and get your response. He was asked on the "Nightline" program how he would teach American history, specifically the Revolution or the Civil War, differently than it is being taught now, and he said that we should teach these events by "focusing on themes which cut across ethnic communities, that find unity within diversity. So if we're talking about the issue of freedom, we can talk about Patrick Henry's "Give Me Liberty or Give Me Death" speech before the American Revolution, but we can also talk about the freedom that is spoken of by Martin Luther King in the *Letter From Birmingham Jail.* "

Raffel: Wait a minute.

DT: He also said, "We can talk about democracy that's expressed in *The Declaration of Independence*, but we should also see democratic ideals in the writings of a Frederick Douglas, the great black abolitionist."

Raffel: This is history thrown into a blender. The man does not sound particularly competent. The whole problem for me in dealing with multiculturalism is not really very complicated, as I'm sure you know. My whole life has been multicultural; I am multicultural. I teach other cultures; I translate from other cultures; I have lived in other cultures; I have respect for other cultures.

DT: Do you think that that's what politically correct persons mean when they use the term multicultural?

Raffel: No, really, they don't. It's unfortunately just slogans. It does not have solid intellectual content. Comparative study of cultures, which I believe in and do, is one thing, but tossing around slogans is something quite different. Slogans really don't mean anything, and you're not educating anyone when all you're doing is filling their heads with slogans. There's no thought. You expect that, I guess, to some extent in younger people, and I was young once, but the way I was taught was that if you said, "A B C is the situation," and someone knows that that is literally not the situation, then they say, "No, you happen to be wrong. It's really C D E," and they show you that this is the case, and you say, "Oh, you're right, and I will no longer go around saying A B C when it's clearly C D E." This is, I think, being educated. But, today, it just isn't working that way. It's all slogans.

DT: Do you also find that you're called names like racist and sexist if you challenge any of the so-called slogans?

Raffel: I've been called sexist, yeah, although I consider myself a feminist. In fact, at the University of Denver, I pioneered a course called "The Feminist Novel in the Nineteenth Century." But I have been called sexist. I was asked to write a review of a book put out by none other than MLA on non-sexist writing, okay. And it was one of the most scandalous pieces of junk I have ever seen. Some woman made a statement, and this is an academic with a Ph.D., and she soberly made the statement that so-called biological differences between men and women are a matter of sexism. So-called biological differences between men and wo-men? So-called? Mind boggling doesn't even do that justice. And they say these absolutely idiotic things. Some PC people, for instance, don't like to use the word "actress". They say that both men and women are actors. They say that actress is a perjorative term. What in God's name is perjorative about it? It's a female actor, and how do you distinguish between a male and a female actor? They say you're not supposed to distinguish. Why not? It's absurd. Now there is prejudice against women; it's certainly true, but that doesn't justify all this other stuff. I have had former graduates of mine tell me, and this to me is incredible, that in job interviews the chairmen of departments where they're trying to get a job have asked them to identify themselves ideologically to see whether they fit with the ideology of the department. Now, this has no place. People's political beliefs or intellectual orientations aren't relevant, so long as they're respectable and honest. The only thing that matters is whether they're the best person for the job. That's all that matters. Or the business of Stanley Fish, who ought to be absolutely ashamed of himself. I don't think he is. Stanley Fish commits what I consider the double sin of not only being a PC tyrant but he's a lawyer, and a lawyer should know better. What he did at Duke University when a traditional, old ACLU type, which is what I am, set up a chapter of the N.A.S. (the National Association of Scholars) at Duke University, Stanley Fish, the chairman of the English Department, actually wrote a letter to a number of people saying that anyone who joined the N.A.S. should not be allowed to sit on tenure and promotion committees and should not be allowed to serve on curriculum committees. This not only sounds like Hitlerism in the name of PCism, but then he didn't even have the courage when he was found out to admit that he had done it, and he denied that he did it. There's no question that he did it, and he attempted to deny it. Talk about morality; there is absolutely no morality in that.

DT: He also said that that organization, the N.A.S., is widely known for its racist, sexist, and, I think he said, homophobic views.

Raffel: This is not only slanderous, it's also a lie. I'm a member of the organization, and I am none of those things. I don't represent those things, and I don't approve of those things. And the reason, quite frankly, that I'm a member of the N.A.S. even though I would say that the orientation of the organization as a whole is significantly to the right of my own orientation, but that is not as important to me as the fact that, oddly enough, this organization, which is, quote, conservative, which is supposed to be a bad word, you know, if you're conservative you're automatically bad, this conservative organization represents what the A.C.L.U. should be representing and is standing up for proper procedures, and freedom of speech, and real academic freedom, whereas these other people are little Hitlers trying to suppress those things. Calling names accomplishes nothing.

DT: Obviously, it's being done at Duke, if Fish's statements can be taken at face value. Do you think that in other places that tenure and promotion are being used against people who don't subscribe to these PC ideas?

Raffel: I don't think so; I know so. Of course, it's being done. There's no question about it. As I said, hiring is being done that way; firing is being done that way; tenure decisions are being made that way.

DT: I did a presentation a couple of weeks ago at the Academic Discussion Group, and when I finished, one of the statements made to me was that history is "nothing but half-truths."

Raffel: A responsible, academic person said that?

DT: A professor said it.

Raffel: A professor said that?

DT: How would you respond to that?

Raffel: With dismay, first of all. It does not cheer me up to hear that. You know the old saying, if you're not careful, you'll find what you're looking for, especially if you begin from a *reductio ad absurdum* position, and these people always find what they're looking for. Certainly, history is not a study of absolutes, but neither is physics.

We begin from the premise that we cannot absolutely know truth, but we have an intellectual and moral obligation to get as close to it as we can, obviously. I am amazed by that, truly amazed. You know, when you're so anxious to prove something that you'll say things like that, which is what these PC people do, it doesn't matter anymore who you are. It doesn't make any difference whether you're a Stalinist, or a Nazi, or a PC person, or a McCarthyite, as far as I'm concerned, it's all the same. This is mud-slinging, name-calling, vicious invective—just awful. Basically, what these PC people are saying is that anybody who doesn't follow the party line is to be put in a concentration camp, and if that isn't Hitlerism, I don't know what is. The funny part is that they say that they're representing "quote" liberal notions; they say they're representing goodness and purity, but if you represent goodness and purity by being a son-of-a-b ——, you're not representing goodness and purity, you're just being a son-of-a-b—— . That's all. It's very simple. If you're calling names, you're a person calling names.

DT: A couple of people said that the difference between PCism and McCarthyism is that McCarthyism was attacking the academy, and PC is coming from the academy.

Raffel: I agree with that. I feel very strongly about the position of the academy in the United States today as it has been evolving because I don't think it has been evolving well.

DT: What would you say its purpose ought to be, and what do you see it actually doing?

Raffel: Scholarship is basically the name of the game. People who are interested in scholarship are interested in pursuing the truth in particular areas of interest to themselves and also in educating the young in those things. Yet, in spite of the fact that we have many, many more universities now and a much larger university population, our country is much less educated, and one of the reasons

for that, to my way of thinking, is that the universities are
not doing their job. One of the ways of verifying that is
to look, for example, at the number of think-tanks between
World War I and World War II. That's a very, very easily
concluded study; there weren't any. You might be able to
find a couple of arguable exceptions, but for the most part,
think tanks are a post-World War II invention. Why?
Obviously, they weren't needed before, and they're needed
now, and they've flourished.

DT: And you regard that as a failure on the part of
the universities?

Raffel: A clear failure on the part of the universities,
yes, and not just the universities but the whole educational
system. I taught my first college class in 1948, and I had
some pretty bad students. I mean, this was a land grant
college where they checked your pulse, and if you had one,
you were admitted. We flunked in the first year I think
something like 63 percent of the people. All the same,
today, the bottom has dropped out of the bottom. The
bottom level today is so much worse than it was before
that it is incredible.

DT: There are those who are committed to the idea
of a core curriculum and a canon and those who are
attacking the canon. Where do you stand on that?

Raffel: It is only when someone is anchored in a
tradition that he is anything. If you're trying to be everything, if you have to represent everything, which is what
multiculturalism seems to mean, that's nonsense. I mean,
I know I'm an American. I dip into all kinds of other
cultures, but I'm an American.

DT: So you accept that there is an American culture
that is different from all others?

Raffel: Obviously.

DT: Is it bad?

Raffel: Not in the least. We should be aware of other
cultures, but we should be aware of them in relation to
ourselves. I lived in Indonesia for two years, studied In-

donesian before I went, and then worked with an Indonesian collaborator eight years before I dared to translate an Indonesian poem on my own, and it was a four line poem, and I got it all wrong. I wasn't born in Indonesia, nor did I grow up there speaking that language with all its assumptions. It's great and all important to become aware of those things, but you have to be yourself first. You see, I suffered from a lot of this when I was younger. I went to Indonesia when I was twenty-five, and I used to call myself a "cultural European" because I was ashamed to be an American, and I cringe a little now when I say that. I must confess that when I went abroad [again] and spent some time there, I not only knew that I was not one of them, I not only knew that I was an American, but I was d—— proud to be an American. It wasn't until I spent time abroad that I realized that America has absolutely contributed something to the history of society. And our contribution is basically that when we look at people we see human beings, not classes or anything else. And that's big and it's important, and am I proud of it, you bet your life I'm proud of it. I'm enormously proud of it. And I finally came back to the United States and specialized in American literature because I finally realized that this is who I am and this is what I am. I can't possibly be anything else. I'm an American. That's who I am. And if that's who you are, then you should be the best American you can be. You don't want to be a fake something else. You don't want to be a hollow thing with slogans and labels that marches to some politically correct set of beliefs.

DT: Arthur Schlesinger's main criticism of all this is that it is, above all else, divisive. It is tearing our society apart. His words were that political correctness and multiculturalism are taking the metaphor of America as a melting pot and turning it into a Tower of Babel.

Raffel: That's absolutely right. Absolutely. That's why I belong to the N.A.S. because the N.A.S., even if I disagree with them, lets me say what I want to say, and they will not object to what I have to say on the basis of who I am.

Stanley Fish, on the other hand, wants me to wear a yellow star. He wants people to wear a yellow star if they don't belong to his group. And I would say that to Stanley Fish's face, and I think somebody ought to say it to him. Somebody's gotta shake him awake. Do we want a society in which in the name of slogans everybody repeats the same, utterly mindless things and we call that unity? That isn't unity. Look, in America, we're a bunch of mutts, and anyone who has worked with animals knows that the healthiest ones are the mutts, and the real dangers are the pure breeds. You pure breed an animal to a certain point and you get a bunch of mongoloid idiots. Muttdom is what the United States represents, and we should be proud of that; we should be enormously proud of that.

This interview is a college colleague of mine who asked not to be identified by name.

DT: I am interested in an episode involving one of your former students. How would you characterize the student's abilities, the student's performance in your class?

Colleague: Okay, that's a more complex question than it sounds because she's not untalented. She has a certain basic intelligence, and she has a great ambition. It's almost as if there were something neurologically wrong.

DT: Was she able to do the assignments that you gave?

Colleague: No, they would always start off in a strong manner, and you would think that it was going to be okay. The first paragraph might be a good introduction or a good strong argument, but very soon it would begin to just go haywire.

DT: In other words, as you evaluate any student's paper, there were some serious deficiencies in the writing itself.

Colleague: Oh, very serious, very serious.

DT: And, as a consequence, the grade was based upon that evaluation.

Colleague: Oh, yes.

DT: And what was her response to your evaluation?

Colleague: Well, I tried to avoid giving her a grade at first because I knew that the minute I did it was going to be confrontational, and I knew that my efforts to help her would be minimized. I wouldn't be able to teach her if she were fighting me. And so I made lots and lots of comments. Her papers are covered with comments, and without giving her an *F* grade I would say, "This paper is unacceptable." And then make suggestions for redoing it, for improving it, and then, when even that resulted in a mini-confrontation, I took her outside one day after class and talked to her very personally, using her first name which I don't usually do, and I said, "If you're going to look at me as the enemy, I can't help you." I tried to stress that I was on her side, that I wasn't the enemy.

DT: So you actually took extra time outside of class to deal with this?

Colleague: Oh, many times, many times and we'd talk about it, and I urged her to let me work with her to make her papers better, and she would sometimes come around. Sometimes she would see me as hero and savior and other times she would see me as villain and Satan. She thinks in very religious terms, too, and so a lot of the notes I got from her would be notes about how I wasn't listening to Jesus and how God had a plan for me and quotations of scripture and then other times how I was vicious and she was praying for me. And other times she would say, "Oh, God sent you to me." It would vary widely. The swings of acceptance were just crazy.

DT: Sure, but what you were concerned about—what class was it?

Colleague: 101. English 101.

DT: So you were concerned about the writing.

Colleague: I was concerned about—yes, about the writing.

DT: That was your primary concern.

Colleague: Oh, absolutely. The writing, absolutely.

DT: The writing process and what comes out of that process.

Colleague: Absolutely.

DT: And that's how you evaluated their work and their performance. In other words, your approach was exactly the same as it has been as you have developed it over the years.

Colleague: Oh, sure. Probably, any difference was that I was putting into place some new wrinkles in my usual system. I was turning at that point more to peer analysis and evaluation and collaborative work and that sort of thing which she could not survive as she could not work in a group because she had to dominate the group. So I had to always be going around and keeping her quiet so that the other members of the group could work.

DT: We're finally at what that class is about. What was her response to your evaluation of her as a writer?

Colleague: Anger. Anger. She wrote me letters all summer castigating me.

DT: Did she suggest that your evaluation was based upon something other than her ability to write?

Colleague: Yes. She blamed it on racist attitudes, claimed that she'd been a victim of racism all of her life, that I was obviously a racist and that she was going to file suit against me for racism. She wrote letters to the *Vermilion* (the student paper) and letters to the *Advertiser* (a local paper).

DT: Were they published?

Colleague: The *Advertiser* published one letter from her, but it did not name me. Then she wrote a letter to the *Vermilion* in which she named a dean who had worked with her far more than I ever did, because the dean had a file on her two inches thick. I mean, she goes back years pulling the same tricks. So she referred to the dean in the letter to the *Vermilion*. I don't think she called me by name.

DT: Did she follow through on her threats of legal action?

Colleague: She carried the threats to Dr. Marotta, I believe, and to the dean. She wrote them letters, and then she drew up some documents that were quasi-legal. She had obviously done them herself . . .

DT: I think I saw those.

Colleague: Yeah, they were crazy; they weren't real documents.

DT: Were they ever filed?

Colleague: No. They were never filed.

DT: She delivered them to . . .?

Colleague: To me, to the dean, to Bob Jones (see next interview).

DT: To the dean? She did go to the administration?

Colleague: I think so. She went to the administration. I'm not sure whether it was the dean, the vice-president, or what, but she did send it to the administration. But they were obviously not valid documents and they were never formally filed. But there was a cover letter saying that she was going to.

DT: And you haven't heard any more since?

Colleague: No. She was seen following me one time. Some graduate students saw her that semester.

DT: On campus?

Colleague: Mm-hmm. I was teaching a course in the library at five o'clock in the afternoon, and so it was almost dark by the time we got out as we got toward Christmas. And so one day I was walking back to my office from the library, and two graduate students, who are still here, saw her following me. They were walking toward the library, and they saw her face. They said they were so struck by the intent of her face and the way she was staring at me that they turned around and followed her because they were concerned for my safety. They didn't know any of this story, but they just picked up on it. And they said when I got back to the building she paused outside the door and didn't come in and, of course, at five o'clock the building's pretty deserted. So they watched her walk away, but they were telling me about it later.

DT: Were you concerned for your safety?

Colleague: Yes, I was, and I started locking my door when I was here.

The next interview is with Bob Jones, an instructor of English at USL.

DT: I want to talk to you specifically about a student, who shall remain nameless, with whom another of our colleagues had a problem. I understand that you also taught this student.

Jones: I did.

DT: But not for the entire semester, is that right?

Jones: Right. I'd say she was in my class for about five or six weeks.

DT: Did you get some writing samples from this student?

Jones: I got three.

DT: Was that enough for you to make a judgment about the student's ability as a writer?

Jones: Very much so.

DT: How would you evaluate the student's ability as a writer?

Jones: As a writer, we'd say someone in need of dire controls. And we'd say pretty good ideas, but she digressed too much.

DT: Not focused?

Jones: Not at all. She defied every rule, every lecture note that I gave regarding what an essay should do. She would begin with an introduction and a thesis, and then for some unknown reason, it was simply just never developed. Paragraph one would say one thing; paragraph two would say something else; paragraph three would say something else, and the conclusion was, "What is this?" When she got her last paper, she actually stormed out of the class. And I was just standing there, and she was walking toward me, and I just stepped aside. What else could I do? And she walked out of the room, and she slammed the door very hard. The one thing I recall very clearly is that she very much disliked being told what to do. Her attitude was, "Don't tell me what to do. I know what I'm doing." She never once said that, but I got that impression. She never came to a conference with me, even after I asked her to.

DT: She wouldn't come to see you when you told her to?

Jones: She wanted class time to be her conference time. You know, "Give me twenty minutes of class time." And I would tell her that we couldn't do that and that she would have to come to conference. Yet, she would still try to manipulate me into conferring with her during class, and I would have to call a halt to it. So, her papers got progressively worse because she wouldn't come to conference.

DT: So you would characterize the student as deficient in writing skills?

Jones: Very much so.

DT: Would it surprise you that our colleague characterized this student in the same way?

Jones: Not at all. In fact, when she dropped my course, she was not doing passing work.

DT: The student said that she had problems in our colleague's class because our colleague was a racist.

Jones: That's nonsense. Had she stayed in my class, I would have done the same thing unless she would have made drastic changes, which I somehow doubt would have happened.

DT: By changes, you mean what?

Jones: Following directions and basically doing what the book and I said to do.

DT: So you would not regard the student's charge against our colleague to be valid?

Jones: Of course not. (Smiling) I wonder what charge she would make against me. (Bob Jones is black.)

DT: The student delivered to our colleague some legal-looking papers. Did you get any such thing?

Jones: I did.

DT: Was it a copy of what our colleague got or was it different?

Jones: I think the cover letter was the same, but I think the actual text was different.

DT: What did it say?

Jones: The student charged me with demeaning her in front of the class. That's basically what it came down to in my legal-like document.

DT: Was this filed anywhere else?

Jones: Not that I know of.

DT: I have found quite a number of examples of students instead of owning up to the fact that they are deficient look for something else to blame, and the charge of racism is one that has been thrown around very loosely.

Jones: I tend to agree. Students basically are becoming what I would call a little too defensive instead of just saying, "Okay, I have a problem; help me overcome this problem." They need to develop a more detached objectivity so that they can say to themselves, "Okay, this is not right. It's a subject-verb agreement error." You know, that kind of thing.

DT: I'm encountering this kind of thing a lot more today than when I first started teaching, and I think it's getting worse. Have you noticed that?

Jones: I have, especially in freshmen.

DT: What is your response to teaching of dialects or allowing dialects to be used in composition classes?

Jones: I tell my students that their racial identity really doesn't matter. I tell them in this type of writing situation, we aim for formal or standard English, which simply negates using particular dialects. I tell them that if they use particular elements of dialect that they must put them in quotation marks to let me know that they know that they are using something that goes against the standards. But I only do that in the first essay. After essay number one, we are to aim for standard usage.

DT: You know that there are people in academia who would call you a racist for saying that?

Jones: We are supposed to make our students collegians. They already know their dialect too well. We're supposed to be training them for their future, and the future is going to make even greater demands on them.

DT: Is there anything you'd like to add?

Jones: I'd like to reinforce this idea of standards, mandatory standards, in punctuation, grammar, structure, and so forth, and they should be enforced.

DT: In the form of grades?

Jones: Yes. Some teachers say things to students like, "If you do all the work, the lowest grade you'll get in this class is a *C*, regardless of the quality." That's lying to that student because eventually someone is going to tell that student, "I'm sorry, this is an *F*."

Chapter 8

CONCLUSION

Unfortunately, the ultimate victims of all the "innovations" and accompanying controversies in public education are our kids, and they are about the only thing still right with the system. The system is failing our kids, and it's just not fair or right. While many adults seem to have learned to live with all the nonsense and with all the excuses as to why things aren't getting any better, that rumbling you may hear in the distance is the resentment and anger of our kids continuing to build. But, as Dr. Oliver Wendell Holmes once said, "The great thing about this world is not so much where we stand as in which direction we are moving." And, if recent history teaches us anything, it teaches us that when young people all get their heads pointed in the same direction, no force on earth can stand in their way. I still believe that we are going to make it; America is going to make it, and we'll make it because of our kids. There is much to be done, but it *can* be done, and that is the important thing to remember.

Many years ago, I went to see a movie called *Lost Horizon*. This was the story of a group of people whose plane crashed in the mountains of Tibet, and just as they were about to perish from starvation and exposure, they were rescued by a bearing party which took them through a maze of secret tunnels which led to an incredibly beautiful valley. Now this valley was completely surrounded by towering mountains and sub-freezing temperatures so that its atmosphere was absolutely pure. Everything here was as it was in the beginning. Here, there was no disease. Here, even aging was a gentle process so that people lived to be a hundred years old. Here, children were respectful and loved learning for its own sake. Here, life was a celebration.

Here, there was no crime, no strife, no suffering. Here, everyone was completely happy and wanted for nothing. And, the name of the place was Shangrila.

During the intermission, I went out into the lobby of the theater for a soft drink and popcorn. There was a young boy standing next to me at the concession counter who was very animated and spoke very excitedly as he pulled on his father's arm. "Daddy," the boy said, "let's go there on our next vacation!"

The father responded, rather sternly and reproachfully, "Stop it. We can't go there; it doesn't exist."

At this, an incredible sadness swept over the boy's face. After a moment of silence, he bowed his head and said, under his breath so that his father couldn't hear, "It can if you want it to."

That is the kind of thinking we need.

Being a true child of the late sixties and early seventies, I *really* bought and internalized all the rhetoric of that period. You know, that "dream" stuff. You know the one, the "dream" that all children "will one day live in a nation where they will not be judged by the color of their skin, but by the content of their character;" the "dream that one day every valley shall be exalted and every hill and mountain made low, the rough places will be made plain and the crooked places will be made straight, and the glory of the Lord shall be revealed, and all flesh shall see it together. . . . And this will be the day—this will be the day when all God's children will be able to sing with new meaning:

My country, 'tis of thee,
Sweet land of liberty,
    Of thee I sing;
Land where my fathers died,
Land of the Pilgrim's pride,
From every mountainside
    Let freedom ring.

"And so let freedom ring from the prodigious hilltops of New Hampshire. Let freedom ring from the mighty mountains of New York. Let freedom ring from the heightening Alleghenies of Pennsylvania. Let freedom ring from the snow-capped Rockies of Colorado. Let freedom ring from the curvaceous slopes of California. . . . From every mountainside let freedom ring."

Now *that's* a dream, and *that's* a speech. But what sadness that we have had to witness such transcendent and inspirational rhetoric of enlightened leaders with a vision reduced to the rhyming clap-trap of manipulative politicians with an agenda, motivated more by ambition than by conviction. They may have the style, but they ain't got the "stuff."

Let us also not forget that, as already mentioned, according to the ideas and rhetoric of PC and all its "isms," Martin Luther King was just another "slave" of the white, European males. That would be especially evident in all his references to Judeo-Christian Scripture and in his references to his own people as "Negroes" and as "Blacks" rather than as Afro- or Afri- or African-Americans. And, of course, his constant reference to America as *his* country makes him a traitor to his African heritage. King also mentions "the magnificent words of the Constitution and the Declaration of Independence." Talk about PNC! Remember, the Constitution is "the embodiment of the White Male with Property Model."

Obviously, what separates the truly inspired and inspiring leaders that I remember from my youth and the PC demagogues of today is that people like King grasped the inherent greatness of the *idea* of America, and they grasped it firmly. And, even though we, admittedly, have not yet lived up to all those high-minded principles which comprise that idea, that is no reason to abandon the effort or trash the idea itself. The idea is that all people, regardless of the surface and superficial differences, can live together and prosper. What is necessary is mutual respect, but the PC crowd has no respect for anyone but themselves. Everything and everyone else, they not only reject, they vilify.

As I said, I *believe* that we are going to make it, and I *know* that America is going to make it because the idea of America is a force that is far greater than any of the petty differences which divide us. As I said in a column I wrote more than four years ago, what this country needs, right now, is not more hot air blowing on the sparks of racial tension which are smoldering everywhere. What this country needs is common ground—understanding, compassion, kindness, respect—common ground where all our people of all colors can stand, common ground where "all of God's children, black men and white men, Jews and Gentiles, Protestants and Catholics, will be able to join hands" and live out the glorious dream that is America.

And, as Dr. King said, "That will be a day not of the black man, and not of the white man, but of man *as* man." Even though Martin Luther King was also very politically incorrect (PNC) in his generic use of the word "man" to mean all of humanity, perhaps even some of my PC colleagues might find it in their hearts to overlook that and consider instead what the man was trying to say.

ORDER THESE HUNTINGTON HOUSE BOOKS !

_____	America Betrayed—Marlin Maddoux	$6.99 _____
_____	Angel Vision (A Novel)—Jim Carroll with Jay Gaines	5.99 _____
_____	Battle Plan: Equipping the Church for the 90s—Chris Stanton	7.99 _____
_____	Blessings of Liberty—Charles C. Heath	8.99 _____
_____	Cover of Darkness (A Novel)—J. Carroll	7.99 _____
_____	Crystalline Connection (A Novel)—Bob Maddux	8.99 _____
_____	Deadly Deception: Freemasonry—Tom McKenney	7.99 _____
_____	The Delicate Balance—John Zajac	8.99 _____
_____	Dinosaurs and the Bible—Dave Unfred	12.99 _____
_____	*Don't Touch That Dial—Barbara Hattemer & Robert Showers	9.99/19.99 _____
_____	En Route to Global Occupation—Gary Kah	9.99 _____
_____	Exposing the AIDS Scandal—Dr. Paul Cameron	7.99 _____
_____	Face the Wind—Gloria Delaney	9.99 _____
_____	*False Security—Jerry Parks	9.99 _____
_____	From Rock to Rock—Eric Barger	8.99 _____
_____	Hidden Dangers of the Rainbow—Constance Cumbey	8.99 _____
_____	*Hitler and the New Age—Bob Rosio	9.99 _____
_____	The Image of the Ages—David Webber	7.99 _____
_____	Inside the New Age Nightmare—Randall Baer	8.99 _____
_____	*A Jewish Conservative Looks at Pagan America—Don Feder	9.99/19.99 _____
_____	*Journey Into Darkness—Stephen Arrington	9.99 _____
_____	Kinsey, Sex and Fraud—Dr. Judith A. Reisman & Edward Eichel (Hard cover)	19.99 _____
_____	Last Days Collection—Last Days Ministries	8.95 _____
_____	Legend of the Holy Lance (A Novel)—William T. Still	8.99/16.99 _____
_____	New World Order—William T. Still	8.99 _____
_____	*One Year to a College Degree—Lynette Long & Eileen Hershberger	9.99 _____
_____	*Political Correctness—David Thibodaux	9.99 _____
_____	Psychic Phenomena Unveiled—John Anderson	8.99 _____
_____	Seduction of the Innocent Revisited—John Fulce	8.99 _____
_____	"Soft Porn" Plays Hardball—Dr. Judith A. Reisman	8.99/16.99 _____
_____	*Subtle Serpent—Darylann Whitemarsh & Bill Reisman	9.99 _____
_____	Teens and Devil-Worship—Charles G.B. Evans	8.99 _____
_____	To Grow By Storybook Readers—Janet Friend	44.95 per set _____
_____	Touching the Face of God—Bob Russell (Paper/Hardcover)	8.99/18.99 _____
_____	Twisted Cross—Joseph Carr	9.99 _____
_____	*When the Wicked Seize a City—Chuck & Donna McIlhenny with Frank York	9.99 _____
_____	Who Will Rule the Future?—Paul McGuire	8.99 _____
_____	*You Hit Like a Girl—Elsa Houtz & William J. Ferkile	9.99 _____

* _New Title_   Shipping and Handling   _____
                                Total   _____

AVAILABLE AT BOOKSTORES EVERYWHERE or order direct from:
Huntington House Publishers • P.O. Box 53788 • Lafayette, LA 70505
Send check/money order. For faster service use VISA/MASTERCARD
call toll-free 1-800-749-4009.

Add: Freight and handling, $3.50 for the first book ordered, and $.50 for each additional
book up to 5 books.

Enclosed is $_____ including postage.
VISA/MASTERCARD#_____ Exp. Date_____
Name_____ Phone: (   )_____
Address_____
City, State, Zip_____